HOW TO WRIT
AND GET IT PUBLISHED

HOW TO WRITE A BOOK AND GET IT PUBLISHED

A complete guide to the publishing maze

Susan Curran

Thorsons
An Imprint of HarperCollins*Publishers*

Thorsons
An Imprint of HarperCollins*Publishers*
77–85 Fulham Palace Road,
Hammersmith, London W6 8JB

Published by Thorsons 1990
3 5 7 9 10 8 6 4

A catalogue record for this book
is available from the British Library

ISBN 0 7225 2146 4

Printed in Great Britain by
Mackays of Chatham PLC, Kent

Contents

Introduction

Each year in Britain, around 40,000 new books are published. Many are written by established writers, but many more are written by people who have never published a book before – and perhaps will never publish another one.

If you have something to write that other people will want to read, and you take the trouble to write it well, then in a year or two your book could become one of the 40,000.

In this book, I – and dozens of other writers, editors and agents who shared their experience with me – tell you how you can make that happen. This is not a creative writing course in any conventional sense: it concentrates on all the practical things you need to know and do in order to get your book written and published. It covers both fiction and non-fiction.

Writing as a business

Perhaps you hope to start out on a full-time writing career; perhaps your only ambition is to write and have published one book. In either case you must set out the whole business in an organized and professional way.

Nothing has done more harm to the prospects of would-be writers than the stereotyped image of a writer as a grandly imaginative soul who floats about the world in a daze, turns in a brilliant but illegible manuscript that is rejected by twenty publishers before being hailed by the twenty-first as a masterpiece, has never heard of deadlines, turns up an hour late (or on the following day) for appointments, and shrugs off any suggestion that he might read his contract or check his tax return. Don't believe it. The writers who succeed are those who are clear about what they want, are determined to achieve it, and set about the whole process with prosaic efficiency.

Most likely you're writing your book in your spare time. Maybe you're none too bothered about making money out of it. The same isn't true of the publishers (or agents) to whom you'll submit it. They are full-time professionals, and they expect the people with whom they do business to behave professionally.

Don't waste their time by being vague or unreliable. Don't invite their contempt by sending them illiterate, badly presented letters and typescripts. Behave to them as you would expect a first-class, highly principled salesperson to behave to you: by always being business-like, courteous, friendly and knowledgeable.

You may not think of yourself as a salesperson, but you must become one if you are to place your work with a publisher. You will be the first person to sell your work, and you must continue to promote it afterwards. Your performance in this role can make all the difference to its reception.

Your expectations

Writing a book and getting it published is a major undertaking. It will take you months or even years. The work is lonely, and you may find it hard to keep up your confidence and enthusiasm. Almost all writers have to cope with rejections. Some never see their work published, and some of those who do find publishers end up disillusioned and embittered when the results don't match up to their expectations.

Why do you want to do it? How long do you expect it to take? What do you expect to get out of it? You're more likely to complete the process and be satisfied with the results if, before you start, you have the best possible idea of what you are taking on and what the rewards are likely to be.

Why do you want to be published?

I nearly headed this section, 'Why do you want to write?' But not everybody who writes wants or needs to be published.

Writing *for publication* is a process of communication: from you, to your readers. It is entirely different from writing poems so full of personal allusions that only you will ever understand them, or a journal as a personal record of your thoughts and feelings, or a novel that you dare not show even your best friend. It demands that you continually consider why your readers will buy your book and what they will expect to get out of it, and that you make every effort to meet their requirements and expectations. If you are not prepared to do this, you should not even consider publishing your work.

Getting your book published can be even harder work than writing it. You will not succeed unless you have not only a desire to put words down on paper, but a strong urge to communicate them to other people.

First of all, you must have something that you want to write about and that other people will want to read. If you have nothing to write about – or if there is no audience for what you want to write – then there is no point in going any further.

Of course, the urge to communicate isn't the only reason why people want to write and publish books. People do it for the money, the fame, to further their careers, or simply for the thrill of holding a bound volume with their name on the cover.

Writers wouldn't be human if they didn't enjoy seeing their books in bookshops and libraries, receiving letters from appreciative readers, and cashing their royalty cheques. They do. But if you want to be recognized by strangers, or to make a million pounds, or to be admired and respected by your friends and colleagues, there are faster and easier ways of doing it than by writing books. Books frequently achieve none of these things. All those motives are understandable, but they're not sufficient. To write for publication, you must want to communicate something.

Why a book?

Even if there's something that you really want to communicate, and you are reasonably confident that there's an audience for it, a book may not be the right medium for your message. What about a television documentary or play? A radio play? A filmscript? Sometimes a book acts as a selling preliminary to one of these, but sometimes it's better to aim initially at, say, a television play, rather than try to squeeze your highly visual idea into book format.

A book holds a lot of words: typically a minimum of 50,000, and sometimes 250,000 or even more. Not everybody needs that many words to communicate what they want to say. Not everybody can manage to use that many words. The idea that you thought would make a novel might, when you start to write, provide only enough fuel for a short story. All you know about beekeeping, how to stop stuttering or the geography of West Wales might fit comfortably into an article in a newspaper, magazine or learned journal.

There's little to be said for starting your writing career with a full-length book. It's rather like setting off on a marathon before you've had any practice in running round the block. Unless what you have to say cannot be divided up into article or short-story size chunks, it's advisable to begin with smaller projects.

True, ten paragraphs in the local newspaper won't look as impressive, or sound as good on your curriculum vitae, as a 500-page blockbuster. But you'll finish it faster, you're much more likely actually to finish it, it's more likely to be published, and it will be published more rapidly than a book would be. Writing short pieces will provide you with most of the rewards of writing long ones, but you'll get them more speedily, more certainly, and lose less if what you write doesn't achieve publication.

When you move on to bigger things, you'll be armed with proof that you can write publishable material. You'll be much more likely than a novice to succeed in placing a book.

Academics invariably work in this way. They build up their reputations by publishing articles in learned journals. Subsequently they may think of expanding one into a book; or an editor, encouraged by their reputation, may approach them with an invitation to write a book.

Poets and short-story writers do much the same. It's almost unheard-of for poets to break into publication with a solo collection in book form. The majority start by placing individual poems in magazines, and many then go on to appear in anthologies before graduating to their own collections.

Poet Gerda Mayer points out another plus when doing things this way round. Few magazine editors like to publish poems which have already appeared in book form, but book editors welcome poems which have appeared in reputable magazines, so this method increases the chances of getting work published several times over.

Finally, many general non-fiction books are commissioned by editors from experienced journalists, and journalists also have the edge when it comes to submitting original proposals for general books. If you've never published a word, no editor is likely to be impressed by your proposal for a hard-hitting biography of Mrs Thatcher, a chatty book about 'finding Mr Right', or a newsy account of a recent war or disaster. Journalists, unlike you, can demonstrate their ability to research and write this type of material.

This book is specifically about writing and publishing books, rather than articles, short stories and other smaller pieces, but do think carefully about whether you're yet in a position to write and sell a book, or whether you'd do better first to gain experience by working on a smaller scale.

How long does it take?

It varies almost infinitely. Some experienced writers can turn out short non-fiction books requiring relatively little research in six weeks. Some romance writers produce one romance a month. However, the small amount of work that goes into these books tends to show. They are instant books, with shelf lives as short as their writing time. They rarely become established as classics or standard works.

Most books take months or years of part-time (or even full time) labour. Non-writers sometimes find this hard to understand. What do you mean, they say, you only write an average of a thousand words a day? How can you do so little?

You can; and do, particularly when you allow for the research, the thinking, the false starts and the revisions. Almost any book takes a beginner longer to write than they expect. This is especially true of fiction.

Publication is also a slow process. On average, allow a year from acceptance of your manuscript to final publication. Some books take two years or even more.

How likely is it to be published?

It depends on the kind of book, and on your skills as a writer and salesperson. A well-respected, highly literate accountant proposing an authoritative and readable textbook on the latest accountancy laws will probably have trouble fighting off rival would-be publishers. Life won't be so easy for the author of a turgid autobiographical novel about a dentist fighting stomach cancer.

Some professionals claim that any book of a high enough standard, with a reasonable potential market, will eventually find a publisher. Others disagree. Many authors received tens or even hundreds of rejection slips when they started out, then went on to become highly successful. Reputable literary agents only try to sell what they consider to be publishable proposals, but many of these receive strings of rejections, and some never sell at all.

Luck certainly comes into it. You only need to find one person – one editor – who likes your book and believes it will sell. Every reader knows that people have different tastes, especially in novels. The first ten editors who read your book may hate it, but the eleventh may love it.

Generally, I believe that if you have a good idea for a non-fiction book, can point to a market for it that isn't satisfied by rival titles, offer it to a suitable publisher, and persuade the editor that you'll be able to produce it competently and on time, you stand a very good chance of being published.

With fiction, the competition is tougher. Competence isn't enough for fiction writers: they need to be outstanding. Fiction is a fickle business, and tastes and fashions can change fast. But success does come to those who submit typescripts that are well written, well presented, have saleable subjects, and are the right length.

Publishers' 'slush piles' of unsolicited typescripts are legendary. Many of the horror stories are all too true. A minute proportion of unsolicited material is accepted. Some publishers can't remember when they last bought anything off their slush pile, though others do regularly acquire titles this way.

Much of this unscreened material is below reasonable publishable standard, and some is of appallingly poor quality. Some would-be authors don't seem to know how many words a book contains: they write far too little or far too much. Many books are badly researched, badly plotted and badly written. Poor grammar and spelling are commonplace. Presentation is sloppy and amateurish. The odds against acceptance are far less daunting if you take away all the hopeless cases, and focus on the competently written, professionally presented typescripts.

However, they are still long. Mills & Boon, the romance publishers, warn the hopeful in their *Guidelines to Authors*:

> The Mills & Boon editorial office receives nearly 4,000 manuscripts for consideration every year from aspiring authors. If a dozen new authors are selected for publication in that time, we reckon we are having a bumper year!

Twelve in four thousand: that's around 0.003 per cent, and a clear warning to those who think there's easy money to be made writing romances. And Mills & Boon are renowned for making positive efforts to attract new authors!

How many copies will it sell?

Less than you think. That's the sad probability. It's common for aspiring authors to over-estimate their sales potential a great deal. It's simply not true that all your family and friends will buy copies. Some will expect you to hand out free copies (and some won't read it even if you do); some will look for it in the local library; a surprising number will show not the remotest interest in what you've done.

You can't take it for granted, either, that a high percentage of those interested in the subject will buy it. Not everybody in your village will buy a village history: at best perhaps one in ten will, though one in fifty is more likely. Not all model railway enthusiasts will shell out for your book about 00-gauge models; not all keen cooks will want to peruse your 500 recipes for lasagne. As for your first novel, it's all too likely that it won't receive a single review, and your local bookshop won't order a single copy.

It's a common misconception that all public libraries buy all new books. What, all 40,000 a year? Even the major city libraries don't take them all. With book prices steadily rising, and library budgets falling, a medium-sized local library may not buy even one copy of all the novels issued by major publishers. They'll perhaps buy 20 copies of the latest Catherine Cookson, but it doesn't follow that they'll buy your book.

Nor do books on popular general subjects necessarily sell many more copies than specialized books. They have more competition. It's true, too, that many publishers make little effort to advertise and market many of the books on their lists. You may find it hard to believe that out of the millions of people who grow roses in this country, only a thousand have paid out for your authoritative treatise on rose growing, but your publisher won't be surprised. As likely as not, they'll have reckoned from the start on selling around that number.

Old-style, hot-metal printing processes made long print runs essential: only for thousands of copies did the volume costs fall to an acceptable level. Today all that has changed, with the advent first of litho presses, then of computerized typesetting, and now of desktop publishing. Some commercial publishers can now make a profit on less than 500 sales, though they'll make a loss, obviously, if they print 10,000 copies and sell only 500 of them.

By way of contrast, a hardback novel rates as a best-seller if it sells 20,000 copies, and so does a paperback that sells 100,000 copies. The top-selling paperback in the UK in 1988 (which was, incidentally, Wilbur Smith's *Rage*) sold just over 480,000 'home' copies (that is, copies published and sold in Britain), according to the *Guardian*'s bestseller list; the hundredth biggest seller (*Flight of the Old Dog* by Dale Brown) sold only 63,000 copies.

How much money will you make?

Again, most likely less than you expect – that is, if you set out to make money out of your writing, which many people sensibly don't expect to do.

There will always be people who try to make a fortune out of writing. It's a job that demands no formal qualifications, no long apprenticeship, minimal capital outlay. It's one of the few ways of making big money (apart from the football pools) that appear accessible to ordinary people.

But nothing is that easy, and hitting the jackpot with your first novel is about as long a shot as relying on the Casino at Monte Carlo to set you up for life. Okay, Jeffrey Archer did it, and received lots of publicity as a result. Thousands of others have tried and failed without ever making headlines.

It'll cost you to write a book. Even if you disallow the value of your time, you'll pay for stationery and postage. You may have research costs; you may need to pay somebody to type up your manuscript; you may have to photocopy it several times (and it'll run to 200 pages at the very least). With many low-selling academic books, the author doesn't even break even.

Many highly-regarded authors of a dozen or more books find that they can't live on the proceeds of their writing. Most of these intelligent, creative, highly-motivated people could earn more money in almost any other profession.

Still want to go ahead? Next you must take a hard look at your idea for a book, to see if it has the necessary qualities for success.

CHAPTER 1

Books that sell

Before you start work on your book, it's worth getting some idea of the market into which you intend to sell it. Then when you begin to develop your ideas you'll be able to emphasize the aspects that will make your book likely to succeed, and to cut out or play down any features that will make it difficult to sell.

First, some hard facts. Of those 40,000 new books published each year, around 5,000 are adult fiction (including romance and other genre fiction), and another 3,000 or so children's fiction and non-fiction. Around 2,000 titles are school textbooks. Other popular subject areas (each accounting for over a thousand titles in a typical year) are art, biography, commerce, education, engineering, history, law and public administration, literature (that is, literary criticism), medical science, natural science, political science and economics, religion and sociology.

The relatively small proportion of fiction accounts for a much larger proportion of overall sales, especially in paperback. Four out of five titles in the paperback bestseller list (the annual Top 100) are fiction.

It doesn't follow that it's easier to get a romance published than a book on marine engineering. Your initial job is to sell your ideas to the publisher, not to bookshop customers. You're competing with other would-be authors, not with books that have already been published. Proportionally more people try to write romances than engineering textbooks. It's easiest to sell yourself as an author if you pick a field with a low proportion of would-be authors to would-be readers.

The list

You'll have heard of publishers' lists, if only through that old chestnut, 'Our list is full.' It's important when planning your book to understand not only what the list is, but how it works, and how it will affect your book's reception.

Virtually every publisher sells two types of books:

- newly published books, and books scheduled for imminent publication;
- previously published books that are still in print.

The entire roster of titles that the publisher has available for sale represents that publisher's list. This can be divided into a forward list (new books) and a backlist (old books).

Publishers produce catalogues of their books, usually twice a year, in which the forward list is invariably given most prominence. Some publishers include part or all of their backlist in their catalogues; some do not. Though catalogues are published twice-yearly, titles are published and sold to wholesalers and bookshops on a monthly basis. Your main concern will be with the forward list: that is, with the list of titles currently in preparation, to which you hope your own book will be added.

The publisher's catalogue is a marketing tool. It goes to bookshops and wholesalers. The publisher's salespeople work from it when trying to persuade buyers to take the month's new titles.

This too is important. A salesperson doesn't go to a book buyer aiming to sell only, say, the latest Catherine Cookson. S/he tries to sell the list as a whole, all the titles which the publisher has available.

Because the catalogue is a marketing tool, it is designed, and the list is ordered, for effective marketing. (This is particularly true of mass-market paperback fiction, but it's true to some extent in every field of publishing.) It starts off with the big titles that will grab the attention of buyers, and that most or all of them are certain to want. (These are 'lead titles'.) The salesperson brings those to the buyer's attention first, and begins – hopefully – with a fat sale. Then s/he works down the list, drawing the buyer's attention to 'support' titles, which are listed more or less in the order of their expected sales.

If the list starts off with a raspberry, that will do nothing for the chances of the books lower down. So it's to everyone's advantage if it contains a good strong lead title or two.

Because the lead titles are so important, publishers prefer safe bets to gambles. A safe fiction bet is the latest title by a prolific big-selling author like Catherine Cookson or Jeffrey Archer. If no book of this certain pulling power is available, the publisher may try to promote an author with a solid smaller-scale reputation, hoping that the lead title will provide their breakthrough into a bigger league. Alternatively a 'big' first novel can, with much hyping, be turned into a successful lead title. But this *is* a gamble, and few publishers would choose first novels for more than one of their top three or four titles.

In a non-fiction list, the lead will again be a 'big book' (perhaps physically, perhaps only in terms of expected sales), probably on a subject of wide appeal, and most likely by a big-name author.

The lower reaches of the list are known euphemistically as the mid-list. This term has spread like the middle classes, so nobody refers to the bottom of the list. Since the early 1970s there has been a discernible shift in balance of sales away from the mid-list and towards the lead titles. Many mid-list titles make little (if any) profit for the publisher, and most publishers' mid-lists have shrunk (either absolutely or proportionately) over this period.

It obviously helps if the publisher's list hangs together as a whole, containing books that complement each other and collectively promote a house image. Often competent books are rejected by a publisher simply because they don't seem to fit the list. Patrick Janson-Smith of Transworld, publishers of Corgi paperbacks:

> There's no point publishing a book unless it actually fits into the programme that we're constantly making up.
>
> There are certain levels. There's the bestseller level, and the big blockbuster, and then there's a second lead title, and then there are the category titles. You can't publish a book in isolation. Although we do occasionally – but 99 per cent of the time with disastrous results.
>
> We've got a sales force who go out, and they're competing against fifteen other mass-market imprints, all say-

> ing, I've got the big bestseller. Our boys are the best in the business in my humble opinion, and reckoned to be so at the moment, but there's only so much they can do. They can't go into a buyer and say, my lead title for this month is X, i.e. the new Jilly Cooper, oh, and we've got three other major books. Okay, you can, but the big chains have only got so much money, and they allocate it.

Building up a list is an art, not a science, and the contents of successive lists from the same publisher may vary greatly, depending on what books are offered to them over a particular period. But generally, the overall size of the list changes only slowly, so it is broadly true that there's only so much room at the top of the list, and only so much room in the mid-list.

Buyers' ratings

Other vital structuring tools in the book market are rating systems such as that operated by W. H. Smith, the largest UK bookshop chain.

These rating systems are based not on literary merit, but on how saleable a book is reckoned to be. In the W. H. Smith system, for instance, a book rated '1' will appear (usually in considerable quantity) in every shop. Books rated 2, 3 or 4 will be stocked in progressively smaller quantities, and in larger branches only, down to a '5' which will merit one solitary copy in the very largest shops.

If a book receives a W. H. Smith '5' rating then its chances of becoming a big seller are virtually zero.

These ratings are carried out *before* books are published, and *before* reviews appear. Those responsible for fixing ratings cannot and do not read every book that they rate. They make their judgements on the basis of the cover, the paragraph or two of blurb in the publisher's catalogue, any information that leads them to expect enhanced demand (for example, a big advertising budget, promises of author interviews in the press or on television, television or film tie-ins, serializations), and their general knowledge of the trade.

Obviously all publishers hope for good ratings for all their books, but these pragmatic judgements are not as eccentric as reviewers' opinions can be, and they are usually in fairly close agreement with the publisher's own assessment of saleability, as reflected in the catalogue layout and publicity budget.

The overall result of this system is that the fate of a book in terms of sales is largely decided before any reviewer pronounces on it, or any individual book-lover picks it up and considers buying it. If your book is placed towards the back of your publisher's list, and if the W. H. Smith buyer glances at the cover and shakes his head, your royalty cheque isn't going to send Jilly Cooper green. Occasionally books are re-rated – for example, if they are shortlisted for one of the major literary prizes (the Booker, the Whitbread and a handful of others) or if the author suddenly hits the headlines – but this is not done routinely in response to the critical verdict the book receives.

What people like reading about

Publishers do comparatively little market research, and most of them claim that the books they publish are so individual that discovering why people bought one book won't help at all to predict whether they'll buy another quite different one. Among the few exceptions are romance publishers. Mills & Boon, who produce more standardized books, rely heavily upon repeat sales from regular readers, and make great efforts to find out what features readers did and did not like in past titles. Some of the results are available to would-be Mills & Boon authors in the form of a tip sheet (obtainable free from the publishers on request) and a cassette, *And Then He Kissed Her*, for which there is a charge.

Most book buyers (and readers) are female, and books that appeal to women, or to both sexes, tend to sell better than books that appeal to men only. (Many editors are women too, and they tend to buy in books they like themselves.) In fiction it helps if there are good strong female characters with whom women readers can identify. There's little to recommend the type of cardboard female who appears in the book only to provide love and sex interest for the dynamic hero, and possesses no characteristics more interesting than her pneumatic bust and her willingness to succumb to even the crudest advance.

When asked what types of books they want, editors tend to become depressingly vague. They all say they want original, well-written books, and their other comments perhaps reflect the styles and limitations of their own publishing houses as much as anything else.

Rachel Hore, an editor at Collins:

> What I look for are books about real people who are *not* in stock situations. I'd like to see more really good strong contemporary and commercial women's fiction; more young experimental writers. They must be original, though, not simply repeating what has been done before. There's also a strong market for good original fantasy.

Imogen Parker, who handled many new authors as a literary agent with leading firm Curtis Brown before joining rivals A. P. Watt:

> It's very difficult to put things into categories and say what sells and what doesn't. At the moment it's quite a good time to sell crime, and it's always a good time to sell really big thrillers, but because of publishers' mid-lists getting so reduced, it's a terrible time to be selling thrillers that are quite good but really not huge.

Patrick Janson-Smith:

> I'm looking for originality. I spend most of my time rejecting books that are yet another Kremlin-based spy saga, evil Russians versus the West. There's so much of that. Unless the writing is captivating and original, there's no point. It's just another book. Even bloody good thrillers are difficult to sell, so a mediocre thriller has no chance. I don't know why, I suppose simply because it's a woman's market.

Does the subject matter of fiction make much difference to its prospects? Opinions vary. Patrick Janson-Smith again:

> I think subject matter's essential, though it depends how it's written. Black Swan [Transworld's more literary paperback imprint] is a bit of a nuisance in a way. You get a lot of people writing in saying, I've written this rather intense

> novel about a social worker in Grimsby or something. Shudder, shudder.

Imogen Parker takes the opposite viewpoint:

> I don't think the subject matter makes all that much difference. I've sold novels with the most gloomy subjects, though they must be really well done. Often those are easier to sell than humorous novels. There's nothing worse than a novel that's supposed to be funny but isn't.

The package

One of the odd features of the book trade is that buyers are in a relatively poor position to judge what they're buying. Somebody buying a bed lies down to see what it feels like; somebody buying a dress tries it on. Wearing it for a month might tell them a little more, but generally they know when they hand the money over what they're getting in return for it, and don't expect surprises.

Book buyers are always surprised. They can't stand in the shop reading great chunks of the book before deciding if it is going to appeal, they have to be content with a quick flick through and a look at the cover. When they read the book it rarely – if ever – turns out to be exactly what they envisaged, and sometimes it's wildly different.

And as I explained above, book *sellers* typically don't read the book before deciding if, and how, it is going to be displayed ready for sale. So the buyers (both wholesale and retail), particularly if they are not already familiar with your work, don't go primarily for your fascinating plot or your scintillating style. They go for a book *package*, of which the ingredients are:

- the story you have to tell, or the information you have to impart;
- the words (and perhaps pictures) you use;
- the layout;
- the cover, including the blurb;
- what they already know about the author and the

book, through free and paid publicity.

All these ingredients are important to every book, though their relative importance does vary from genre to genre.

You must bear this in mind, not least because publishers are accustomed to the idea of selling book packages, of which the author's input is only one part. (And sometimes, their manner implies, a pretty minor one.) When you submit a book to a publisher, it will be judged not only on the text (which may not even be written at this stage) but on an assessment of what you as author can contribute to the package.

Similarly, when you settle on a publisher for your book you need to assess not just the money on offer, but the publisher's style of production, their taste in covers, the efficiency of their sales force, and all the other factors that will influence the sales of their book packages.

It's galling enough for an author to face up to the fact that many people decide to buy (or not buy) a book not because of the quality of the prose, but because of their opinion of the cover. It can be even more galling to realize that what the publisher assesses in the first place is less the text on offer than the author who is offering it.

That's the hard truth. Typically, the author's personality and qualifications count for more in the package than does the text.

Attractive authors

If you're trying to find a publisher for your first book, then it stands to reason that you're not already a best-selling author. That's tough. Publishers like best-selling authors best of all.

But they can't publish only best-selling authors, and second-best, in their eyes, is an author who has the potential to become a bestseller.

Some would-be authors are famous already – as politicians, film stars, newspaper columnists, famous sportsmen, television celebrities, you name it. They have an enormous advantage. The public are much more likely to buy their book than yours, *however good yours is*. They are the odds-on bets to become the next generation of best-selling authors.

Patrick Janson-Smith again:

> I bought a book by Julie Burchill the other day. I read it and thought, it's disgusting, wonderful, I'll go for it. This is sex 'n' drugs 'n' rock 'n' roll, but she puts it together very well. And you've got Julie Burchill, the woman they love to hate. I was thinking about that all the time.

Julie Burchill didn't only find a publisher for her first book, she had it chosen as a lead title by a major paperback house. This won her an advance (that is, a down-payment) and guaranteed publicity on a scale that most first novelists would kill for. Her book will most likely be rated '1' by W. H. Smith; it will appear in shops that bottom-of-the-list novels won't appear in; it is much more likely than the average first novel to become a bestseller.

Okay, you are (most likely) not Julie Burchill. But your prospects will improve if you can demonstrate, even on a modest scale, any of the advantages that tip the scales in favour of people like Julie Burchill. Any or all of these points will count in your favour:

- You're stunningly attractive.
- You have a memorable personality (like David Bellamy, Magnus Pyke, Janet Street-Porter) that comes across well in the media.
- You are the kind of pushy extrovert who will do anything, but anything, to promote your own book.
- You are a relative or intimate friend of lots of famous people (or just of one very famous person).
- You can point to anything about yourself (preferably, but not necessarily, connected with your book) that will attract publicity.

Cynical of me? Maybe so – but realistic. All these factors are likely to impress that W. H. Smith rater who won't have read your book.

Today's authors are media personalities. Books sell because people get to know about them, and they get to know about them because of the publicity they get. It's easier for a book to get publicity if the author is 'good publicity material'. That's true today not only of pulp fiction, but of Booker prize-winners, cookbooks, d-i-y manuals, even serious academic tomes. Look at Shere Hite, the beautiful author of *Women and Sex* and other sociological sex studies; look at Stephen Hawking, disabled best-selling author of *A Brief History of Time*. They wrote good books (and that is a small but necessary requirement for success) but they also provided good publicity for those books.

Score zero? Your chances of hitting the big time have plummeted, though there's no reason to despair if you're hoping to be published on a less splashy scale.

More prosaically, publishers like writers with outstanding qualifications for writing on their particular subject. You don't need merely to be an expert; you need to *prove* that you're an expert. If you're famous, this is easy. It seems that people will believe what famous people write about almost anything. But if you're not famous, you still gain points for credibility:

- if you are a senior academic in a relevant (or at least slightly relevant) subject – preferably at a major university, though the local poly is better than nothing

- if you have deep and extensive experience of whatever you plan to write about. One year's experience (of a job, a foreign country, whatever) is much less impressive than twenty, thirty, fifty years' experience. The more dramatic and unusual your experience, the less of it you need. (One earthquake, one spell as a castaway on a desert island might do; one divorce, one cancer operation doesn't have the same cachet.)

- if well-known people in the same field vouch for your expertise. (It's necessary to tell the publisher about them, and this, of course, entails asking their permission first.)

- if you have already written on the subject, even if it's only an occasional column in the local newspaper or a small circulation magazine.

Finally, though you may not yet be remotely famous, you may have the potential to become famous in future – as a writer! It *is* still possible to do that, even if you're not Julie Burchill.

The vast majority of best-selling authors – of both fiction

and non-fiction, though this is especially true of fiction – are long-established ones, with many books to their name. They have armies of fans who already know their work, or at least their name. Good sales are virtually guaranteed for everything they write. Wilbur Smith, Catherine Cookson, Frederick Forsyth and the rest didn't start out famous, they became famous by writing books.

Sometimes it happened with their first book (it did for Frederick Forsyth, for instance) but not always. But whether they hit the big time instantly, or built up their reputation over years, the appeal for publishers lies in the fact that these authors are *regular producers*. Their cumulative sales are vast, not least because they have written lots of books.

Not all authors are as famous as these. Publishers are also happy to keep on authors whose sales are moderate but reliable, though with the shrinking of the mid-list times are harder than they used to be for the journeyman author.

Publishers like prolific authors. These authors gain regular reviews and publicity which keep their names in front of the public, and produce regular new titles with which to excite jaded booksellers. Repeat business is welcome in almost every field, because bigger profits come from the follow-up orders. And publishers are only happy to budget for a small loss on a first, second or even third novel (as they often do, since they know that many, many novels by relatively unknown authors make a loss) if they expect to be rewarded with comfortable profits on subsequent books.

Even in these days of short shelf-lives and instant financial returns, many publishers still take this long-term view. Obviously they can only do so if they have every reason to believe that the author will keep on writing books regularly.

Patrick Janson-Smith yet again:

> It's absolutely essential that an author should produce regular books. The author I'm happiest with is the author who gives me a book a year. Glorious. And the ones that do are making it. Mary Wesley is a perfect example, she's done a book a year. *Not That Sort Of Girl* was a bestseller, but her first four books were not.

It's worth remembering that Mary Wesley began writing novels very late in life. Even so the quality of her work, and the hope that she would produce a string of novels, made her a saleable proposition.

Non-fiction packages

In non-fiction book packages the subject matter is generally the largest element, though this isn't invariably true. It helps again if you as author are a saleable personality. It helps if you arrange your material sensibly and put it across clearly and entertainingly. It helps if the book is well laid out, illustrated and produced. But it's primarily the subject that determines how well the book will sell. (And the price, but that's another story . . .)

Biographers see this particularly clearly. Even the best known biographers find that their books sell far more on their subjects' reputations than on their own. Historical biographer Jasper Ridley has written about a wide range of sixteenth and nineteenth century subjects. His book on Garibaldi sold disappointingly in the UK, though it was a bestseller in Italy: even this very famous foreign statesman didn't excite potential readers. In contrast, his biography of Lord Palmerston did extremely well here, but much less well in the USA, where Palmerston is a less familiar figure.

There's no stage in their career at which biographers can indulge themselves by writing about interesting minor characters, Ridley laments: when they start, publishers complain, 'Who'll want to read a book *about* someone nobody has ever heard of written *by* someone nobody has ever heard of?' while when they are established, publishers insist, 'We want a *big* book from you, a Book Club lead title. You'd be wasted writing about an unknown cleric. How about a biography of Henry VIII or Elizabeth I?'

Photographer and writer John Hedgecoe finds the same problem:

> General books sell better than specialized ones, which is obvious anyway. So publishers do all tend to want to make every one a general book, which isn't as interesting to do as a specialized book.

However, there can be a danger in going for too wide or popular a topic if you're a young and unknown writer. Your proposed biography of Henry VIII would compete with Jasper Ridley's biography – and probably lose out, since you aren't as well known. Your biography of an interesting minor figure would be much more likely to have the field to itself.

The credibility factor also favours books with limited topics. If the great British public have never heard of you, why should they think you the ideal person to write *The Ultimate All-Purpose Cookbook*? You'd find it easier to impress them with your credentials for writing (say) *The Cheese Cookbook*, or an even more specialist title. A dozen cheese cookbooks on, you'll start to look like the right author for a cookery blockbuster.

Controversy

Publicity – good or bad – sells books. If you as an author don't (yet) readily attract publicity, perhaps you can write a book that will.

Biographer Albert Goldman wrote a hard-hitting biography of John Lennon, *The Lives of John Lennon*, which received extremely critical reviews, not least because of its sensational allegations. Relatives and associates of Lennon, including Paul McCartney and Yoko Ono, urged readers not to buy it. It sold so well that it figured in the bestseller charts for several weeks.

Novelist George Target achieved much the same result on a slightly more modest scale:

> I used to be a teacher and I wanted to expose teachers. Teachers are a lot of frauds in my opinion. Call themselves professionals, most of them couldn't teach a pussy how to drink milk. So I wrote a novel called *The Teachers*, and I realized that if I irritated enough teachers they would cause a tremendous controversy and it would sell a lot of copies. And they weren't bright enough not to do it.
>
> Instead of ignoring this book they all blasted it in the teaching trade press which gave me the opportunity of responding in letters and so on, and I carefully stirred up this controversy. It sold about 75,000, which was extremely good for a novel in those days.

Novels that don't sell

George Target's career as a published novelist came to an

abrupt end when he finished up a series of novels on aspects of contemporary English life with one that satirized the publishing industry. *The Triumph of Vice* (a gloriously misleading title which markedly ups his Public Lending Right returns) did get published, but none of Target's 11 subsequent novels have been accepted.

Over the years, he has produced a remarkable anthology of 'What Not to Write a Novel About':

> I wrote a novel about nine years ago called *The Magdalen Affair*, which was a love story between Jesus Christ and Mary Magdalen, where Mary Magdalen actually has Christ's child. No one would touch that. And I wrote one about animal lovers, pointing out that animal lovers are more fearful than animal haters because they only love animals. They haven't much time for human beings. I've written a thriller called *Chalice of Blood* which is about press barons taking over the media. There's no earthly chance of that book being published.

Fortunately Target doesn't mind too much about not being published: he's happy to keep on writing the books he wants to write, and isn't interested in making compromises.

Other subjects novelists should avoid? Rachel Hore of Collins:

> We tend to receive far too many thrillers. There simply isn't a market for all of them. We also receive too many books which are based around 'the story of my divorce' or 'how I got over a death'. Many of these writers seem to be concentrating more on getting an experience out of their system – which, of course, is an excellent thing to do – rather than on writing something new and original.

Thrillers again: everybody agrees that there are too many thrillers. Agent Imogen Parker adds:

> Too many of the thrillers start with a man on an aeroplane, coming in to land. Invariably he's incredibly handsome and the beautiful air hostess is making eyes at him.

Imogen Parker's other dislike is books that the author describes as:

> 'a sort of thriller but it's got a bit of humour and there's a

romantic element'. One sort of wonders if they know what they're doing. It sounds immediately as if they haven't got control over the material.

Genre fiction is here to stay, and life is easier for would-be authors who manage to be original within the genre boundaries, than for those who try to break through them.

Originality is essential, though, even in writing romances for Mills & Boon. True, there are only a limited number of basic variants on the boy-meets-girl theme, and they've all been done before: but at the very least individual characterization, an original sub-plot or an unusual background ought to make *your* book a little different from all the others.

Please, please don't write a novel about a struggling writer trying to write a novel. And don't assume that a string of funny incidents that happened to you and your friends, lightly fictionalized, will add up to the plot of a humorous novel. They won't.

Generally only famous authors can get away with very short novels. It's inadvisable to fall below 70,000 words. Some would-be novelists imagine that the converse is true: the longer a novel, the more likely it is to appeal. It's expensive for publishers to produce doorstep-sized books, though, and unless they foresee a sizeable sale they're also likely to despair at the sight of your 250,000-word-plus masterpiece.

There isn't much of a market for books of short stories by well-known writers, and there's virtually no market for books of short stories by unknowns. Though poems that have appeared individually in magazines can successfully be collected into book form, there's less scope for doing this in the short story market.

Non-fiction that doesn't sell

There's only a small market for poetry in book form. Many poetry books are published even so – often by very small presses – but nobody should assume that there's money to be made by writing poetry. There isn't.

Few people buy biographies or autobiographies of people they've never heard of, and far too many people write (or at least, try to have published) their own life-stories. Memoirs go hand in hand with fiction in making up the bulk of every slush pile. James Herriot and Laurie Lee notwithstanding, it's extremely difficult to publish your memoirs successfully unless you're already famous.

The same goes for books that focus on any personal experience – for example, keeping pigs, converting an Elizabethan farmhouse or rowing across the Atlantic – that falls short of grabbing the headlines. Most people are simply not interested in knowing what you did unless you can describe it outstandingly well. They may react differently if you use your experience to give depth to a 'how-to' book. So consider writing *How to Convert an Elizabethan Farmhouse* rather than *How I Converted My Elizabethan Farmhouse*.

Unless you're famous, it's unlikely that many people will wish to read your personal opinions and ideas on politics, philosophy or religion, however original (or genuinely impressive) they may be.

Non-academics generally find it difficult to sell books on fundamentally academic subjects. Even for popular historical biographies and children's histories, publishers like an author to have solid credentials as a historian.

It's difficult to sell a medical book unless you're a doctor. It's next to impossible to sell a book about philosophy, economics or psychology unless you have recognized academic qualifications and the endorsement of academic specialists in those fields. You may feel that all the academic economists are on completely the wrong track and your personal theory is much more sound, but few if any publishers will risk losing the respect and trust of the economic establishment by publicizing your maverick ideas.

Finally, some books sink because they lack international appeal. This is particularly important for big, highly illustrated books: cookbooks, photography handbooks, gardening books and the like. These books are so expensive to produce that they *must* generate big sales, preferably spread over editions in several languages. A British edition alone is unlikely to generate much profit.

Often the likelihood of an American edition makes all the difference to a decision whether or not to publish. Americanized spelling isn't a problem: a copy editor can easily adapt that. But if all your examples focus on British laws, customs or geographical locations, the appeal to an international market may be drastically reduced, and you could well blow your chances of publication.

Don't despair, however: every rule has its exceptions, and books by the most unlikely people, on the most unpromising subjects, have in the past become unexpected successes.

CHAPTER 2

Developing an idea for a book

Before you can write a book, you must know what you're going to write about. That may sound obvious, but it isn't always so.

Every book starts with an idea. Everybody has ideas, and writers arguably have more than most people. But not every idea makes a good basis for a book, and it isn't always easy to recognize those that do.

The best idea for a book is:

- *An idea that interests you*. If you're not interested in it, how can you expect anyone else to be? Even if a publisher is begging you to write the authoritative book on the history of Mongolia in the ninth century, or the implications of the new Social Security Act, there's no point in agreeing unless you are genuinely interested in the subject. If you are not, the writing will be a chore to you, and the book you write is likely to be boring.

  The prospect of a fat advance often makes professional writers deeply interested in the most unlikely subjects. You know best how much motivation you need, and of what kind, to carry you through a long project. For a first book, though, it's wiser to pick a subject that already interests you, than to assure yourself that the interest is sure to come when you get to work.

- *An idea that interests other people*. Before submitting your idea to publishers, try it out on friends and colleagues. Choose people who you think are potential buyers of your book. Are they genuinely enthusiastic, or polite but lukewarm? If you don't sense real enthusiasm, why not? Think hard and honestly: would the book you have in mind interest enough people sufficiently strongly to persuade them to buy it? Or might it be too obsessively focused on your personal beliefs or experiences?

- *An idea that's original* – or, at least, fairly original. A little originality is often better than too much.

It obviously isn't sensible to suggest writing a book that's very similar to a recently published title, but publishers tend to be wary of truly offbeat ideas, because unusual books are gambles for them. An adult novel with badgers as the main characters? A diet book that concentrates on slimming hips and thighs? Okay, these particular books (Aeron Clement's *The Cold Moons*, Rosemary Conley's *The Complete Hip and Thigh Diet*) made it big, but only after many publishers showed sublime disinterest in them.

'Original' to a publisher often means a small variation on what is already proven to be popular. Mills & Boon say that they want new writers to have a recognizable voice of their own, but it has to be a Mills & Boon kind of voice: radical new approaches are definitely not welcome.

Publishers like originality best when it is combined with a safe bet – as in books about new gadgets, major news events, and leading contemporary characters. When the home-computer market boomed in the early 1980s, fast-acting authors and publishers did well out of 'how to use your computer' (and 'which computer to buy') books. Publishers wanted cookbooks about microwave ovens and food blenders soon after these first appeared; they wanted biographies of Sarah Ferguson after she announced her engagement to Prince Andrew. Obviously lots of authors suggested titles along these lines, and only the best qualified won contracts; lots of books were published, and few of them became bestsellers.

If you are an expert on a subject (and you have no business writing about it unless you *are* an expert at least in a small area), you should know whether – and where – there is a shortage of books. If your fellow teachers groan that there's no suitable up-to-date textbook for a widely taught class; if you have scoured the bookshops in vain for a specialist (but not too, too specialist) book on your hobby; if your experiences and knowledge are of proven interest to other people, your subject will come to you ready-made.

Beware of bandwagons. Books take a long time to write and publish. That vogue for medieval whodunnits or books called 'making the best of your camcorder' may be past history by the time your offering is ready for the presses.

- *An idea for which there is an adequate market.* It may interest you and your Aunt Molly, but will it interest ten thousand other people? Five thousand? Or only five? And how easy will it be for the publisher to identify, and sell the book to, that very small proportion of the population?

  Publishers don't publish only books with guaranteed huge sales, but they can profit from small print runs only if they succeed in estimating sales accurately. You have a real advantage if you can identify the market for your book clearly, and a bigger advantage if you can suggest how to target it – for example, by advertising in a specialist magazine, through direct mailing to members of a society, or through intensive publicity in a small area. Selling 1,000 copies of a town guide to Bradford is much easier than selling 1,000 copies of an experimental novel.

  You, and not your publisher, know most about the audience for your book. Maybe you want to write a book about 00-gauge model railways. You probably belong to a model railway association. Most likely your potential publishers won't know the first thing about model railways, but if they read, 'Fifty thousand people belong to 00-gauge model railway clubs, and as a member of the Model Railway Association I have access to a database of their names and addresses,' their enthusiasm will shoot upwards.

- *An idea that appeals to a publisher.* Publishers don't

always get it right, but no book that failed to find a publisher has become a bestseller.

Of course, your idea is more likely to appeal to a publisher if you pick a suitable one to submit it to, present it well, and convince the publisher that you can write an authoritative, interesting, readable book.

Publishers also have ideas for books. Ian Graham, technical writer:

> Despite having written over 20 books, I have never been able to persuade a publisher to take up an idea of mine. I've had some very pleasant meetings with many, many publishers, editorial directors and editors, but in the end they go ahead and publish books that *they* want to.

How do you persuade the publisher to ask *you* to write that book? See Chapter 3.

The idea for a novel

When Frederick Forsyth was a foreign correspondent, working in Paris in 1963 at the height of the OAS attempts to kill Charles de Gaulle (there were six actual attempts, plus a number of abortive plots) it occurred to him that the reason why the plots all failed was because the OAS was too thoroughly penetrated by French counter-intelligence. The French knew all the OAS hit-men. But what would happen, he wondered, if the OAS hired a foreign professional assassin who was not known to the intelligence forces?

This simple 'what if' idea sparked off his first best-selling thriller, *The Day of the Jackal*. All of Forsyth's subsequent thrillers have started in much the same way, with a one-line idea. What if a young German journalist decided to hunt down a vanished Nazi? What if? What if?

Forsyth's ideas can come from almost anywhere: from a conversation, a magazine article, a television documentary. They take root, and he mulls them over. (He thought of that original idea for *The Day of the Jackal* in 1963; it wasn't until 1970 that he began to write the book.) Is it original enough? Is the plot feasible and believable? Is there enough of an idea to make a whole book? Ideas that pass these tests go on to form the basis of books.

Novelist Jeremy Leland works in much the same way:

> I read a small article in the *Irish Times* about a fisherman and his two sons whose fishing boats capsized in a storm on Lough Ree, an extremely large lake on the Shannon. They were wearing life jackets and were bobbing about in the waves when a passing cruiser with a young couple on board saw them and altered course to rescue them. But the sides of the cruiser were steep, the couple were inexperienced and lightly built, the sodden fishermen were heavy, they could not manage. In despair the couple left them and motored flat out for Athlone to get help. Too late, of course, all three were drowned. I visualized the would-be rescuers struggling, failing, and having to make that awful decision, and thought I'd like to explore the horrific experience because it was so unusual. I knew the Shannon well, having taken boats up it several times. And once as a teenager and poor swimmer I'd fallen overboard from a sailing dinghy and thought my last moments had come as it sailed away.

Leland started to turn the incident into a short story, but 150 pages later he still hadn't reached it, and thus there came about his first published novel, *A River Decrees*.

Judith Lennox-Smith, whose first novel *Reynardine* was published in 1989, got the idea for her plot from a folk song. Not all novelists have the same approach. Historical novelist Cynthia Harrod-Eagles, author of the *Dynasty* series:

> I usually start with the characters. If I know who they are and what they're like, then the plot naturally arises from their characters. Usually either one or two characters suggest themselves immediately. It's not really a matter of working them out. I suppose that must be what I'm doing subconsciously, but on a conscious level they appear to me already to exist, and I just suddenly see them for the first time.

Pat Barr, who writes historical novels (*Chinese Alice, Kenjiro* and others) set in the East:

> I think for me it's usually an historical situation that sets me

> off, rather than perhaps any kind of emotional conflict. One develops that later. I never write about famous people. They may be off-stage, and I may have quotes from them and their lives, but I'm not interested in them. I'm interested in the way that history and historical events shaped the lives of ordinary people who got caught up in it in various parts of the East, in the nineteenth and early-twentieth century.

Kathy Page, author of *Island Paradise* and two other novels:

> What I start off with is a really strong sense of structure, but it doesn't actually have the plot in it. I know it's a bizarre way of doing it, but it's almost like painting. I have a strong idea of what kind of writing, what person it's going to be in, if it's going to cut between past and present – that sort of thing, which is a lot of what interests me about a book, anyway. So I start off and I think, it's all going to be in the present tense, and I'm going to cut between these two situations all the way through the book. There's an underlying conflict, but I don't focus on the mechanics of that conflict.

Many novelists, like Page, see the development of their image as an almost visual process. Paul Scott, writer of the *Raj Quartet*, wrote a fascinating essay called 'Imagination in the Novel' in which he works out the way in which his novel *The Birds of Paradise* took shape.

He begins with a visual image, that of a woman appearing in a doorway. Slowly the image of the woman becomes clearer to him, and he senses that she is unwell – or perhaps just too hot. Is the novel going to be set in a hot country? But he doesn't want to write a novel set in India, where he has already located several: he wants to write a novel set in Spain.

As he returns to the idea of Spain, the woman acquires a name, Dora. She is coming through the doorway into a room, and in the room is a man, Bill. Scott begins to doodle, drafting possible opening sentences involving Dora and Bill. But these are abortive: he doesn't yet know what story he wants to write, or how he will write it.

He thinks of Dora and Bill as travellers, with lots of luggage. They wear fine feathers. That phrase sticks, and becomes a symbol. He thinks of the fine feathers of birds of paradise; he begins to research birds of paradise. And slowly – there's much more exploration of the process in the original essay, which is well worth reading – the idea of a novel called *The Birds of Paradise* begins to emerge.

Clare Lavenham who writes doctor and nurse romances for Mills & Boon, tends to start with a setting. As she finds it tedious to keep to hospital backgrounds all the time, she tries to think up other locations in which doctors and nurses might meet. She particularly likes to write about nurses attached to countryside general practices.

This is a common approach amongst romance writers, who need to find exotic and unusual backgrounds against which to set love stories. Elizabeth Oldfield, another leading Mills & Boon writer, travels extensively in her search for original and authentic settings. She decides on a setting first, then racks her brains for a reason why her hero and heroine might be there. The conflict that is the core of the story often emerges quite naturally from this reason, though sometimes she will come up with a storyline first, and finds she has to set the book in London, say, in order to fit it.

Reference points

Many novelists find that their idea crystallizes in their mind when they think of a title for the book. A good title should focus the theme of the book, or identify the central character. If you don't have a title in mind, it is easy to lose track of what you mean the book to be about, and to go rambling off down side-alleys.

Similarly, many writers who don't use full synopses (discussed later) find it helpful to start with reference points in their head, ideas of where the story is going. Kathy Page:

> I have some sense of what starts it all off and where it gets to, but then there's a lot of unknown territory in the middle. I start with probably about three points that I want to get to. I normally know the end. I'm sort of an end person.

George Target, prolific novelist who also runs a class in creative writing:

> When I was writing a novel every year, I used to write the first paragraph on the back of a Christmas card on Boxing

Day. By, say, the end of August I would get to think about what I was going to write next. I had the whole book planned, without a word on paper, by about Christmas. Boxing Day after dinner, it was a little ritual, I'd take the biggest Christmas card I could find and I would write the first paragraph.

In all the novels I've had published, I've stuck on the first page the first written paragraph. It doesn't alter very much from the printed one.

I would try also, at the same time, to write the last sentence. I use this technique in the class. If you can think of a first sentence of a short story and the last sentence, the story writes itself. There's already a spark in the mind that goes between the two.

The first sentence is often extremely important, not only to the development of the idea, but for selling purposes. It's essential to have a striking opening if you plan to submit your novel cold to a publisher or agent. Perhaps only the first page will be read: if you don't grab the reader's attention there, it's too late.

My own first novel, *The Mouse God*, became clear in my mind – and acquired a title – when I hit on a first sentence. I knew I wanted to tell the stories of three women caught up in the fall of Troy. In researching legends of the Trojan War, I learned that one of these women, Chryseis, was the daughter of a priest to a shrine where Apollo was worshipped as God of Mice. This idea came to fascinate me. The mouse struck me as a very odd choice of sacred animal. Suddenly my opening came to me: 'Chryseis was in her third summer when she first let out the sacred mice.' I knew what the core of my theme would be, and how the mice would act as a metaphor for what I wanted to say: how the book would start, and how it would end too.

Reading up the opposition

Once you have a general idea of what your book will be about – and before you begin to plan it in detail, let alone to write it – you must research the immediate market into which you hope to sell it.

All the best writers (and most mediocre ones) are also

voracious readers. Most likely you've already read lots of books that fall into the same broad category as the one you plan to write. If not, you must do so before you go any further. You can't hope to produce a book that people will want to read unless you know which books people *do* read. You can't aim to do better than the opposition unless you know what the opposition has done.

Some people set out to write kinds of books they've never read themselves – for instance, to write a Mills & Boon romance or a 'shopping and f***ing' blockbuster when their preferred reading is Tolstoy or Iris Murdoch. The only ones who succeed are those who, one, research the market thoroughly by reading lots of similar books; and two, find that they actually *enjoy* the books they read.

Only if you understand what draws readers to books in any genre can you hope to put those ingredients into your own book. Cold-hearted writing to a formula rarely if ever works. Even if you've read a hundred thrillers, historical romances or gardening books before, you must research the field now. You'll be looking at books in a different way now that you are a potential writer.

Some writers argue that it isn't a good idea to read other people's books while you're writing your own, either because it will break your concentration, or because it may tempt you to plagiarize other people's work. Whether or not you read while you're writing is up to you. You must read, though, before you begin to write.

Yes, plagiarism is a risk, and you must be conscious of the danger of it, and make continual efforts to avoid it. But it's much more of a risk if you read only one similar work to the one you're planning, than if you read a hundred.

Many hard-up readers obtain their books primarily from local libraries, second-hand bookshops, at jumble sales and car-boot sales, or from market stalls. There's nothing wrong with that, but do go into bookshops selling new books as well. If your budget is tight, you can make a note of titles then ask the local library to order them for you. The writers of newly-published books have around a two-year lead on you: books in libraries and on second-hand stalls are often much older. You must be aware of new trends, since in every field, fiction and non-fiction, the characteristics of successful books tend to change.

Romances provide a good example. Even over the last five years, there have been noticeable changes in the preferred types of hero and heroine, and enormous changes in the amount of sex required. A romance reader who depends (as many do) on buying books second-hand might not appreciate that the 'sweet' romance with no explicit sex has lost most of its market. Heroines today are not promiscuous, but they generally go to bed with the hero before (sometimes well before) the end of the book.

You can't read too much at this stage. If you're planning to write a romance, read a hundred or more. A long historical novel or spy thriller? Read at least twenty. A non-fiction book in a clearly-defined field? Try to look at every book that is in any way a rival to yours, and read cover-to-cover at least half a dozen. Spread your field if you find it hard to track down that many successful titles.

Your first aim will be to get a solid overview of your field. Then you must analyze the opposition in depth.

Select half a dozen titles, and take a long hard look at them. What's good about them, and what less good? Which aspects of their writing or production would you like to see imitated in your book, and what would you hope to do differently?

Ask yourself questions like these:

- *Who published it?* Do you like the style and standard of the production? Would you like to be published by the same firm? What nationality is the publisher? What nationality is the author?
- *How similar is it to your planned book?* Might your book fit into the same series? Might yours complement it well in a publisher's list? Or is it so similar to your book (for instance, a rival textbook for the same course or a biography of the same person) that yours would do better with a competing publisher? (Or is it so very similar that you'd do better to forget your idea and look for a new one?)
- *How long is it?* Count the pages. Count the illustrations, if there are any (a rough count will do if there are lots). Count the words on a page (a couple of pages will give you a reliable figure unless the book has mingled text and illustrations, when you may need more) and

multiply by the number of pages to get a rough overall word count. Publishers think in terms of thousands of words: so should you.

If you are thinking of submitting a book for an established series, it will have to fit that series in length as well as style. Standard Mills & Boons, for example, are always between 50,000 and 55,000 words long. There's no point in writing a longer one: at worst it will be rejected, at best you'll have to cut it down.

Even for a one-off book, you need to be able to give an idea of its likely length to publishers or agents.

As a rough guide, a novel with around 200 pages generally contains 70–80,000 words. A blockbuster or a fat textbook might contain 200,000 words or even more.

- *What do you think of the writing style*? Is it formal or chatty? Is it clear or obtuse? Is it well suited to the intended audience, juvenile or adult? Which aspects of it would you like to imitate, and which would you shun?

For non-fiction books:

- *Is the material well arranged*? Would you plan to arrange your material in a similar way? (Chronological? by subject area? starting with an overview and going on to cover specific points?) Or would your arrangement differ? How?
- *How is it arranged* – in chapters, sections, subsections? Do you plan a similar arrangement? If not, how will yours differ?
- *Is the coverage adequate*? Are there major areas that the author hasn't covered, but that you will? Are there areas in the book that yours won't cover? Might potential readers perceive this as a weakness in your book?
- *What reference material (index, glossary, bibliography, footnotes or endnotes) has been included*? Is this sufficient?

For fiction, a casual read-through will have told you what story the author has to tell. Now think hard about the strengths and weaknesses of the plot. Are there points at which your attention sagged? Why? Are there points at which your belief in the story wavered? Why? Do you think enough happened? Or too much? Was it always clear what happened?

Did the book grip you quickly, slowly, not at all? Was the end satisfying? If not, why not?

Look at how the story was told. For instance:

- *Is it in the first person (a main character speaking as 'I') or the third person*? If in the third person, from the point of view of which character or characters? (Which characters do you follow through the scenes? Whose thoughts are you told about, and who do you see only from the outside? Which characters did you empathize with?)
- *Did you find all the characters believable*? If not, why not?
- *How many main characters are there*? Did you find them sympathetic? If not, did this affect your enjoyment?
- *What timespan does the story cover*? How does the author handle the passing of time, and any large gaps within the timespan?
- *What proportion of dialogue is there? What proportion of static description (e.g. of characters' appearance and clothes, of scenes)? What proportion of action?*

Take a close look at a few chapters – perhaps in the middle, rather than at the very start – and analyze the scene structure. How many incidents are there? How many changes of physical scene? How much space is given to each incident? How does the author handle the transition from one scene to the next?

Fixing your format

Now you should be ready to think about your own book.

Try to visualize the book as you would ideally like it to appear. How many pages? How many illustrations? What kind of cover? Which publisher?

Now ask yourself what is the least you would accept. Would you mind if your book came out in paperback only?

(Or if it came out in a hardback library edition, but not in paperback?) Maybe you'd like to include 500 photographs, but would you settle for only 100? Would you settle for line drawings instead? Or agree to do without illustrations completely?

Perhaps you'd like a big glossy tome with a dustjacket, but would you settle for a slot in an established mid-market or down-market series? Ask yourself now. Don't rule out the possibility of compromising later, but do fix your own requirements firmly in your mind before you begin negotiating with publishers.

CHAPTER 3
Publishers and agents

You should now know which publishers produce your type of book. The next step is to make a list of those you plan to approach. Omit any foreign publishers unless you have a very good reason for including them.

It may seem pessimistic to draw up a list, when you hope to be accepted by the first publisher you try. But it will save you work, and help to keep you going, if you receive an initial rejection or two. And if you do receive a rapid 'yes' from the first publisher you approach, you may find it wise to check with at least one other publisher before accepting their offer, to see if they could offer you better terms or a more attractive overall deal.

If there are plenty of publishers in the field, include around five on this list. There are not always five you can include. For instance, there are few alternative markets for romances written for Mills & Boon. No general fiction publisher is likely to take them, at least without a major rewrite. Rejected Mills & Boons look to other publishers like rejected Mills & Boons.

When dealing with general (middle-brow fiction and non-fiction) books, many authors and agents start by approaching major publishers (for instance, Collins or Random Century). These firms are geared to big sales; they (sometimes) pay big advances. If the reaction is lukewarm, you can move down-market and try smaller firms.

You may want your book to be published by a specialist firm, or think it more likely to appeal to one. If so, start with them. It makes sense to try a religious publisher if you are writing a religious book, and to choose a publisher with a sizeable technical list if your book is highly technical.

The safest publishers to try are those whose books you

have checked out while doing your research. If you list a publisher whose books you haven't seen, you should check that they do publish books in your field. The *Writers' and Artists' Yearbook* and *The Writer's Handbook* (see Bibliography) give a very brief indication of which firms do what. If that isn't enough to tell you whether your book might fit their list, then phone the company and ask.

All too many would-be authors send their submissions to unsuitable publishers. If you submit a novel to a publisher that handles only non-fiction, or a romance to a firm that focuses on highbrow literary fiction, you're wasting everybody's time.

How publishers find writers

While you are looking for a publisher, publishers are looking for writers. It may help you to know how they generally find them.

Often, publishers generate their own ideas for books, and then commission authors to write them. Sometimes they generate the ideas very precisely, by planning a series of books, fixing the length and format, deciding what the titles will be, and then looking for an author to write each title. *The Oxford History of England*, for instance, naturally divides into the Thirteenth/Fourteenth/Fifteenth Century and so on. Each title has a different author, but there are similarities in approach and coverage (fostered, naturally, by OUP's editors), as well as in the presentation of the volumes.

Sometimes publishers' ideas are looser. The series format might be fixed, but the content of individual books more fluid. For example, Myra Schneider was commissioned to write books for a series Heinemann produced for reluctant teenage readers. The format and limited vocabulary were fixed constraints, but Schneider's story, *If Only I Could Walk*, was her own.

This is a common approach in juvenile fiction, and for 'how to' kinds of book, where a series like 'Made Simple' may be added to as and when good ideas materialize. Other publishers brainstorm ideas for their list without being certain which one of them will eventually lead to books – or in what format. This book arose in that way. The idea and title originated from the publishers, Thorsons, and I was invited to prepare a synopsis suggesting how I would handle the subject. So the actual coverage and presentation of material were left to me.

Publishers also suggest ideas to their existing authors, especially in non-fiction. So a biographer like Jasper Ridley for instance might be asked, will you do another book, please, and why not make it about Henry VIII? Though publishers naturally talk over fiction ideas that their authors come up with, they rarely generate very specific ideas for fiction.

Publishers can only commission authors whom they know about. Their existing tried-and-trusted authors obviously have an inside line to this type of contract. New authors are found via agents; through personal contact; by approaching universities, polytechnics, trade organizations, specialist magazines, and any other likely-seeming source; when they write in and suggest themselves.

The last route may sound like a last resort, and often it is, but it can work. Authors who write to a publisher suggesting that they write one title may well get a response on the lines of, no thank you, but how about writing this one instead?

It doesn't hurt to mention in a covering letter that while you are offering the publisher, say, a biography of Lord Kitchener, you are an expert on the First World War generally, and willing to consider writing other books in that field. It doesn't hurt to tell the publisher of a series (perhaps of children's fiction) that you would like to write for it, and to ask if you might discuss ideas with them. They may not come up with a firm commission by return, but at least you'll know you are writing the kind of book that they want to receive. (Conversely, you'll know if the series is about to be discontinued, or if somebody else has been commissioned to write the title(s) you were thinking of.)

Work that is firmly commissioned (that is, the author receives a contract) is normally published, but not invariably so. Sometimes the writer and the publisher disagree on the brief, or the publisher doesn't like the work when it is delivered. Editors leave and their successors have different ideas; publishers occasionally go broke. Life is still better for an author with a contract, though, than for one writing entirely on spec.

If it's true that publishers tend to publish the books they want to publish, rather than the books authors want to write, it's also true that authors regularly manage to persuade publishers that the book they are writing, or have written is just what the publisher wants.

In other words, publishers receive submissions from authors. Some of these are no more than sketchy ideas; some consist of long synopses; some comprise complete books, ready for publication, or perhaps already published in a different format or different country.

Publishers get these submissions through several different routes:

- *They ask for them*. They talk to authors – who they may meet socially, or at specialist conferences, or who they know because they already publish them – find out what the author is writing, has written or is planning to write, and express a willingness to look at it. These are effectively solicited submissions.
- *Other publishers send them*. It is common for publishers to offer some of the 'rights' in books to other publishers. Hardback houses may offer the paperback rights to a paperback house (or, increasingly, vice versa); US publishers offer the Commonwealth rights to a British publisher; foreign publishers offer translation rights. (There's more information on rights and international markets in chapter 8.) Many publishers, particularly mass-market paperback houses, obtain much of their material this way.
- *Literary agents send them*.
- *Authors send them*. These are unsolicited submissions, which form the 'slush pile'.

No submissions are accepted automatically, but some are much more likely to be accepted than others. Publishers are generally biased towards buying subsequent books by their existing authors. They look carefully at material that is submitted by agents and publishers' rights departments with good reputations. They generally give a much lower priority to the slush pile.

What this means, typically, is that a new novel sent in by an existing author will not be rejected until it has been read through two or three times, by in-house editors as well as freelance readers, while a novel taken off the slush pile may be rejected after a freelance has glanced cursorily at the title page. If the title page survives the cursory inspection, however, then the slush pile offering will be read just as carefully as – perhaps more carefully than – the existing author's novel before being accepted.

With the slush pile offering, the whole process is likely to take longer. Submissions move to the top of the pile only slowly, and it can be six months before your work receives that quick once-over.

Publishers have no financial incentive to consider submissions received from agents and rights departments more favourably than they consider unsolicited submissions. If anything the reverse is true. Agents generally extract better terms for their clients than unrepresented authors ask for themselves. The only reason why material received through these routes gets better treatment is that it is generally of higher quality. These are books that have already been sifted once. They may have already been published; at the least an expert considers them to be of publishable quality. Not all of them will be accepted, but all of them deserve taking seriously. Alas, this isn't true of the slush pile.

The proportion of books that publishers take from the slush pile varies considerably, but it is generally in the range from zero to ten per cent of their total acquisitions.

Collins, publishers of general fiction and non-fiction, plus the Collins Crime Club, publish around 50–70 hardback novels a year. Of these, perhaps one a year will come from the slush pile. Thorsons (independent until acquired by Collins) are non-fiction publishers, with an emphasis on practical books, health books, 'new age' books, aviation and military books. They have three main imprints, and reckon to receive between 1,000 and 1,400 submissions per year, per imprint – around 3–5,000 submissions overall. The entire division publishes around 300 titles a year.

Of the submissions that are accepted, approximately 65 per cent are existing books. Around 30 per cent of these are identified and followed up by Thorsons themselves, either from mentions in *Publishers' Weekly* or from the Frankfurt Book Fair. A further 35 per cent are unsolicited books sent in by foreign publishers; 20 per cent of acceptances are of material sent in – unsolicited – from literary agents; and 12 per cent or so are books commissioned from authors, from ideas generated in-house. That leaves around 3 per cent – typically six to ten titles a year – that are taken from the slush pile.

Romance publishers Mills & Boon actively encourage amateurs to write for them, to the extent of suggesting it in their books. But in a typical year, they will only accept around twelve typescripts from the slush pile.

Paperback houses like Corgi take very little unsolicited material. Patrick Janson-Smith is adamant that they do look at the slush pile, though 'inevitably not too critically, because of the pressure on people's time'. This type of publisher is not oriented towards working with authors to fine-tune promising manuscripts, and a book with possibilities is more likely to be steered towards a hardback publisher, from whom the paperback rights may subsequently be bought.

M. E. Austen sold his novel *Love-Act* to Jonathan Cape – the first publisher he sent it to – through the slush pile. Kathy Page sold her first novel, *Back in the First Person*, to Virago on her second attempt. Judith Lennox-Smith sent her historical romance *Reynardine* to Hamish Hamilton, on the advice of an agent who did not take her on as a client. They accepted it.

So it *is* possible to break into print this way. If your work is good enough, and suitable for the publisher you select, it will be accepted – and quickly. But anything you can do to move out of the slush pile, and into a different entry route that will lead to closer consideration of your typescript, is to your advantage.

How the slush pile works

Every publisher has slightly different working practices, and here I can only give one or two examples.

Collins – one of the largest British publishing houses – receive on average 50 or 60 unsolicited submissions a week, though there is seasonal variation, and the number can rise to 80 or 90 a week in the spring. The total is well over 5,000 a year. All of these are sent first to a freelance reader who sifts through them.

Collins' current reader reports that the contents of the slush pile are broadly representative of what Collins publish, with a bias towards war reminiscence, memoirs, historical fiction, and – as usual – thrillers. There is very little 'literary' fiction: perhaps people who write novels about ideas tend to find a literary agent. At one time he plotted the rejects geographically, to produce a Map of Authorial Submissions. There was no particular pattern: writers from all over the country send material.

In two years reading unsoliciteds, Collins' reader has found two books which have been accepted. Very few submissions are of publishable standard. Some are very good, he reckons, and might be acceptable to other publishers.

He reads very few typescripts from beginning to end, reckoning to tell from a fairly brief glance whether or not something has possibilities. 'Sometimes one reads so little,' he says, 'because the quality is not very good.' He is conscious that his work does not pay for itself in terms of his 'finds': Collins, like most other British publishers, see considering unsolicited submissions partly as a public relations exercise.

The vast majority of submissions – around 99 per cent – do not get past the freelance. Those that do survive this first sifting are submitted to Collins' staff editors.

There may be 50 or 60 of these possibilities a year, and each one is now read more carefully. A large majority of these too are rejected, either because they are not quite up to standard, or because they are thought more suitable for a different publisher.

In some publishing houses, freelances are not used, and in-house editors scan the slush pile. Otherwise, Collins' procedures are broadly representative of how general publishers operate.

Mills & Boon, a more specialist firm, receive around 4,000 unsolicited submissions a year, so the success rate (assuming a dozen are accepted) is around 0.003 per cent. The company publish only romantic fiction, and normally to a standard length of 50–55,000 words. Work that does not fit this formula stands no chance.

Mills & Boon claim that unsolicited submissions receive precisely the same treatment as submissions sent through literary agents (and this is generally agreed to be true). They claim, too, to read every unsolicited typescript, but that does not necessarily mean that they read it from end to end. However, work that shows promise *is* read carefully, and many would-be authors receive long letters with suggestions for improvement.

This seems to be a general characteristic of slush piles, in fact: that much more work than is ever likely to be accepted, is read carefully and seriously considered. Where work is *not* seriously considered, it is because the editor or reader rapidly becomes convinced that it is either unsuitable for the list, or not of publishable standard.

Escaping from the slush pile

For the aspiring but unpublished author, there are only two ways to avoid the slush pile. You must either make personal contact with your potential publisher, or find a literary agent.

Contacts

They help – in fact, they help massively. If you already know somebody in a suitable publishing house, you have a very good reason for choosing to submit your book to that publisher.

Computer expert Erwin Schneider offered his *Multiplan User's Guide* to John Wiley, a major publisher of computer books, because he had an acquaintance working there. They accepted it. Jan Morrow offered her non-fiction children's book, *Child's Play* to Longman because her husband had once written for them, and still had contacts there. They accepted it, and she went on to write an entire series of books for them.

Schneider and Morrow were fortunate: their acqaintances were working for suitable publishers. Your own contact might work for a publisher who isn't ideal for your book. Even though the publisher accepts it, you may find subsequently that you might have received more money, won larger sales, or had your book published more impressively, with a different firm.

There's much to be said for concentrating on making acquaintances at the publishers you feel will be best for your book.

Though this may seem difficult, it's not impossible, even for those who live outside London. People involved in the book trade do meet each other. Publishers are perpetually on the look-out for potential authors. All you need to do is to place yourself in their way.

Many writers find writers' circles and writing courses (not the correspondence kind, but evening classes, university courses, short residential courses) helpful for providing them with contacts. You may not immediately meet a leading editor in your field (though many writers' circles *do* invite publishers to speak to them), but you stand a very good chance of encountering other writers who know editors and agents.

Kathy Page placed her first novel from the slush pile, but she was subsequently recommended to an agent by novelist Zoë Fairbairns, whose creative writing course she had attended. Juri Gabriel, writer and literary agent, runs a course on novel writing at Morley College, London. He not only acts as an agent for several of his students, he has also helped them to set up their own small publishing house.

Professional writers' organizations can be excellent sources of contacts. Norman Leaver writes books for children, including *The Cannon and Ball Annual*, and *Inspector Gadget* stories. Though he is based in Manchester, he finds The Writers' Guild and The Society of Authors (which has a specialist children's writers group) extremely helpful. Through their meetings and conferences he meets publishers as well as other writers. Once he has made contacts, he can phone and discuss the work he might do, before sending in a proposal that is carefully tailored to the publisher's requirements. This is vital when you write, as he does, for established series. However, this is a route for the partly established: you cannot join either organization until you have, at the least, a contract for your first book.

Cookbook writer Josephine Bacon (*Exotic Fruit*, and several other titles) recommends book fairs. These are often open to members of the public. The books on publishers' stands indicate where their interests lie; by talking to the staff manning the stands, she has made the first steps towards book contracts.

If you have sufficient chutzpah, you can go and meet publishers at their offices. Frederick Forsyth got his first break this way, after *The Day of the Jackal* had been rejected by four publishers. He bluffed his way into an editor's office at Hutchinson, and 'snowed him' into reading a 20 page synopsis of the novel then and there. Three days later he was discussing a contract for three novels.

Telephoning first is a more practicable route for the faint-hearted. Perhaps because they are submitting words, many writers seem to think that their first approach to a publisher should be in writing. But publishers, like people in other professions, do most of their business by telephone these days. Few of them object to being phoned by a would-be author. Patrick Janson-Smith, Transworld:

> I think any bold approach works, if it's a good idea. If someone rings me up and says, "This is my novel," I usually, being a soft sort, say "Send it to me." They've got my name and I've spoken to them, and I feel a definite obligation to get the book covered, even if I don't read it myself. But the answer is going to be no if the answer is going to be no.

Kate Allen, Thorsons:

> I'm happy to get phone calls from would-be authors. Their chances of success are improved, and I can give them feedback on what I'm looking for. But if people push too hard, it can be very off-putting.

There's a fine line to be drawn between a bold approach and a desperate one. And never, never take this line before you have a really good, well-thought-through proposal to put forward. If you hustle hard and then submit a turkey, you'll find it much more difficult to be taken seriously the next time round.

If you still prefer the thought of an initial letter, then at the very least you should find out the name of a suitable editor to send it to. (Again, consult the *Writers' and Artists' Yearbook*, or *The Writer's Handbook*; and if you need to, phone up as well.) Even if the submission will be read initially by a freelance rather than your addressee, this indicates that you have done your homework properly, and helps to give a professional first impression.

Agents

First, the bad news. Agents have slush piles, too. Those with no contacts are at the bottom of the queue to acquire an agent, and anything you can do to build up your contacts will repay you.

But do you really want an agent? Publishers tend to say 'yes'. Rachel Hore of Collins:

> Get yourself a good agent. Agents act as a filter on a massive scale, and work that is accepted by an agent has a much better chance of being accepted by us.

Some authors agree. Suzan St Maur, non-fiction author of *The Home Safety Book* and other titles:

> Overall, I think literary agents are worth their weight in gold; most of them work damned hard for their 10 per cent, and earn every penny of it.

Not everybody concurs. Novelist Jeremy Leland was told by publishers Gollancz, after they bought his first book, that he should get an agent. He took their advice, and his agent then proceeded to sell his next three books to Gollancz, on very similar terms, and pocket 10 per cent commission on each one. In retrospect, Leland takes a rather dim view of this advice. Photography writer John Hedgecoe doesn't have much time for agents either:

> I did have an agent once, but he was fairly useless, as most agents are, I think. They don't do anything you couldn't do yourself.

In fact, though many of the authors I have talked to use agents – and most of the successful full-time ones do so – most of them expressed far more dissatisfaction with their past and present agents than with their publishers.

What agents do

Basically, they sell your work for you. They send submissions to publishers on your behalf. They negotiate the advance payment and the contract terms. They may sell different rights in your work (paperback, US, translation, film) individually, whereas without an agent you would trust your publisher to deal with rights for you. (Publishers take a hefty rake-off, generally larger than an agent's, in recompense, though they may give you better terms initially if they are granted all rights.)

The agent will act as your representative in any dealings or disputes you have with the publishers. S/he will receive payments due to you from the publishers, and account for them to you.

Agents also provide you with a contact in the publishing world. When a publisher is looking for an author to write a specific book, s/he will often approach agents to see if they have any suitable clients.

Some agents – but not all – offer editorial advice to their clients, and play a major role in shaping and developing their writing careers.

What agents look for

This is largely dictated by the fact that literary agents charge a fixed percentage of their client's earnings. If they sell a novel to the first publisher to whom they submit it, for an advance of £100,000, they will pocket £10,000, with the prospect of more to come. If they sell a novel to the seventeenth publisher to whom they submit it, for £500, they will pocket precisely £50 – most of which will be swallowed up by postal costs.

So agents like to handle authors whose books can be placed easily, and will sell in good quantities. Note that I say authors rather than books. Even more than publishers, agents look for authors with whom they can work over a succession of books.

If you are planning to write one book only, of a relatively specialized or esoteric nature, it is not worth your while looking for an agent. No successful agent will find you to be a worthwhile client.

Similarly, if your book has already proved hard to place (suffering, say, ten rejections) then no agent is likely to be interested in you.

As a rule of thumb, an agent won't make a profit from a

client until s/he earns at least £10,000 a year from writing (and some like to double that figure).

The cynical say, and with some truth, that agents only agree to handle work that could be placed easily without an agent. That's understandable. A bad book is a bad book. If it arrives on the publisher's desk accompanied by an agent's letter, it will still be turned down.

Many aspiring authors feel that agents would be wise to give them more editorial advice, so that they can turn their bad books into better books. Agents are hampered in doing this because it is generally considered bad form for them to charge a fee for reading and commenting on submissions. If you want advice on how to improve your writing, you would do better to attend a writing class.

Some agents do give editorial advice to some writers. They do so partly out of interest (most agents, like most publishers, genuinely like books), and partly because they believe their effort will be repaid with a saleable book and a profitable long-term business relationship. Both of these motives are necessary: agents are not charities for the succour of hopeless would-be writers. Agent Imogen Parker:

> If you're not going to take something on and really get involved with it, there's no point in making constructive criticism. Not unless you really feel that there's something that will work about it, and you could see something in the future coming of it. Or if you felt that with a small amount of work, or even a large amount of work, there would be something terrific. Then one would make criticisms.

The pluses and minuses of using an agent

- The minus is obvious: *it'll cost you*. Agents typically take 10 per cent on British sales (though a minority charge 15 per cent), and 15 or 20 per cent for foreign sales, where sub-agents are often involved. So you will only earn around 90 per cent of what you might otherwise have earned.

  Out of this cut, the agent has to pay the costs of an office (generally in or around London); endless phone calls; postage of heavy manuscripts; lunches consumed by editors, and sometimes by authors, too. Few agents get to be rich. Those that do, often rely heavily for income on a few star clients who effectively subsidize the less exalted.

- There is a related plus: *you can hope to earn more*. A good agent knows the market far better than the average author. S/he knows which editors are looking for which books, and doesn't waste time submitting proposals to the wrong people. S/he may put work your way that you would not otherwise have been offered. S/he should be better than you at negotiating an advance. S/he should know all the standard contract pitfalls, and make sure you avoid them. So you will – hopefully – get more money, sooner, with fewer snags.
- *The agent comes between you and the publishers*. Some people find this a minus. It's not always easy for an author with an agent to build up a close relationship with an editor. It's your agent, not you, who gets that phonecall – and that business lunch, too.

John Hedgecoe (who no longer uses an agent):

> I think publishers love having a personal relationship with an author. They don't like the agent in between. They suffer them, but I don't think they like them.

There can also be personality clashes between editors and agents. Aggressive agents in particular are offputting to many editors.

- On the plus side: *if you have a dispute with your publisher it's helpful to have a professional on your side*. If you feel you could get a better deal from a different publisher, an agent will be able to help you negotiate a change. If your editor leaves your publisher when you're halfway through writing your book (it happens so often that some authors now write an 'editor' clause into their contracts, which allows them to follow the editor) your agent can provide welcome continuity.

In general, relationships between authors and their agents tend to be longer and more continuous than those between authors and editors, particularly in non-fiction, where many authors write for a variety of publishers, and only the agent has an overview of their career. An agent can also provide a helpful *second professional opinion* on work that is causing difficulties.

Monies that come via an agent inevitably take a few days to be processed through the agent's office. But when money does not come from the publisher when it should (and some publishers are terrible about paying all the money that is due on time) the agent is in a stronger position than the author to *press for payment*.

Finally, it's no good looking for an agent if you're the type always to feel that you could bark louder yourself. Historical and romantic novelist Cynthia Harrod-Eagles, author of 26 books (some published under pseudonyms):

> I got my agent after book seven. I didn't actually want one. I'd always worked on my own, and I'd negotiated contracts and felt happy doing so. But a publisher/writer friend who got me my first commission was quite insistent that I should have an agent, and that I wouldn't progress any further unless I had one. Since I'd always regarded him as my professional mentor, I took his word for it. He recommended an agent to me, and I wrote off with a list of books I'd published so far and what I was doing at the time, and he offered straightaway to take me on. But I'm not entirely convinced it was the right thing for me. I think I'm much too independent. I like to do my own negotiating. We sometimes come into conflict over that, because he wants to be the one round the table.

John Escott, writer of children's fiction:

> I need to be in close touch with my work. When I had an agent I used to send her a manuscript and not have a clue what she was doing with it.

How to find an agent

It's regularly claimed that there is a shortage of good literary agents, when compared to the number of writers who would like to be represented. But successful writers generally have no difficulty in finding agents. It's the potential clients on whom the agency is likely to make a loss who find it hard.

It's necessary to sell yourself to an agent, just as you would if you were approaching a publisher direct. Your chances will be enhanced if you can use personal contacts, rather than approaching the agent cold. You need to come across as an efficient, sensible, personable author. You need to sell your book as a good business proposition. Vague and amateurish approaches do not work.

It is just as necessary to choose the right agent to approach, as it is to find the right publisher. And it's harder, because those outside the literary world generally have little feeling for the reputations of different firms.

The *Writers' and Artists' Yearbook* and *The Writer's Handbook* provide annotated lists of the main agencies, though they can give only a very general idea of the acency's style and reputation. The Society of Authors will make suggestions to its members on agents to approach, with an emphasis on those who are prepared to take on new clients.

Some agencies are general, and some specialize. Some handle mainly fiction, or mainly non-fiction. Big agencies may seem safe options, but some tiny firms are highly regarded: Carol Smith and Deborah Owen run outfits which they choose to keep small, but which have excellent reputations.

Of the major agencies, Curtis Brown, A. P. Watt, A. M. Heath, Peters Fraser and Dunlop, Aitken and Stone and David Higham Associates are all generally reckoned to offer safe pairs of hands. (This is not an exhaustive list, and not intended to denigrate agents not mentioned.) However, these leading agencies are not always the best homes for aspiring unknowns. Suzan St Maur:

> I would personally stay away from the big famous agents, unless your book is certain to be a bestseller. They just don't have the time to devote to giving you the encouragement you need. Smaller agencies, and new ones looking for fresh talent, are the best bet, and apart from becoming good friends and encouraging allies, they're prepared to hustle on your behalf a lot more than if they had Freddie Forsyth and Jeffrey Archer on their books.

One-man, part-time agent Juri Gabriel (who disarmingly describes himself as 'a sort of marginal person, rather like a Fourth Division football club') successfully sells work for a variety of clients whom he has acquired through personal recommendation and his creative writing class. (Like several other small agents, he doesn't list himself in the writers' handbooks). His forte isn't million-dollar transatlantic deals, but he has pushed some of his clients' advances up to the five-figure level. Above all, he offers sympathetic encouragement (combined with criticism where it's needed), a range of media contacts, and what he describes as 'permission to succeed' for authors who, like most, need a boost to their self-confidence.

Though small agents can suit authors well when they do hustle, not all the less well-known agents are rising stars and some seem to do precious little hustling. Technical author Ian Graham, author of around 20 books on computing and similar subjects:

> I've had three agents. All three had very good reputations and were highly thought of in the business. None of them managed to sell a single word of my work. One of them almost bankrupted me by insisting on an exclusive agreement whereby I could not look for work myself.

Most reputable agents do not insist on this type of agreement, and you would be unwise to accept such a condition unless you are very confident that you have chosen correctly.

CHAPTER 4
When and how to sell your book

With non-fiction, you should start selling as soon as you've done your basic research – or even sooner. If you have publisher or agent contacts or both, you can mention what you're thinking of writing – and see what the reaction is – when your book is no more than a vague possibility. However, if you're planning to accost an unknown publisher or agent in person, by phone or by letter, it's as well to have a good submission already prepared (details below) so that you can move quickly to back up your initial approach while it's fresh in their mind.

Not only do you not need to write a non-fiction book before finding a publisher for it: it's actually better if you don't – for the publisher as well as for you. You avoid the heartache and expense of spending months writing a book that nobody wants; they get a chance to comment, and to adapt your initial suggestions so that the book fits their requirements.

This is the professional approach: to offer a complete typescript looks unprofessional.

If you've never written a book before, this system may make you apprehensive. Will you be able to write it acceptably? Publishers rarely worry about this. They are buying an idea, planning a book package of which your prose is only a small part. If you or they do have any doubts, these can usually be resolved by your writing a few (up to three) sample chapters.

Fiction is different. It's harder to write, and would-be authors with good ideas don't always come up with good books. Nor do books that start well always end well. Publishers will not normally buy a novel on the basis of a synopsis and sample chapter unless the author has already published successfully. There are exceptions, though, and Mills & Boon, for example, will happily accept this kind of submission, though they may not sign the contract until the book is completed.

So if you're writing a first novel, it's as well to finish it before you think of selling it. (In fact it's as well to finish it, set it aside for three months, read it through to see if you still find it as good as you originally hoped it was, and only then think of selling it.) The same is true of poems, short stories and autobiographies (unless you are famous).

The initial approach

You have (if you've been following my advice) already decided who to approach. What you do next will be much the same whether you approach an agent or try a publisher direct. However, don't ask an agent if they will *publish* your book. Agents get annoyed with authors who imagine that they are publishers. They are not, and they cannot promise you that a book they handle will be published, though they will do their best to place it with a publisher. Ask instead if they would be prepared to represent you.

It's wise to start with a 'feeler' approach. Meet and talk to, telephone or write to your contact. Tell them that you are thinking of writing (or have written) a book, and describe it and yourself concisely – that is, in no more than three paragraphs, or their spoken equivalent.

For fiction, you will spend two of those paragraphs on the book, and mention:

- *The genre.* This *is* helpful, even if you don't feel that your book is entirely typical of a genre. If your book is basically a thriller, even though it has comic elements, then call it a thriller. If it's a novel that will appeal mainly to women, or to men, say so.
- *The period, contemporary, futuristic or historical.*
- *The plot, ideally in a one-sentence summary.* (If you find this hard to envisage, try reading the blurbs on the back of a few paperbacks.)

- *The approximate length*. The paragraph on yourself will mention any previous books or stories you have had published, and any promotable features of you as an author (your unusual age, your fame as a Page Three Girl, or whatever).

For non-fiction, spend one to two paragraphs on the book. Mention:

- *The broad subject area*.
- *Roughly what sort of book you envisage*, for example, the length, number of illustrations, overall arrangement.
- *Your reasons for believing that there is a market, and a gap in it*.

Also make it clear how far you have progressed with the book. Then spend one to two paragraphs on yourself, concentrating on your qualifications for writing the book.

Finally, if you have approached other agents or publishers simultaneously, it is necessary to mention this fact. There is no need to send return postage with a short letter or synopsis. However, publishers and agents naturally prefer you to enclose return postage with a complete typescript.

Take care over this approach. Draft and revise a letter until the working is smooth; make notes in advance of a phone call, so you can be sure of mentioning all the important points. Present it professionally. Make sure that you give your name (your real name, even if you plan to write under a pseudonym), address and daytime phone number.

Timing is important. Don't accost a publisher who is already late for another appointment. Don't phone at 4.30 on Friday afternoon, or at 9.00 on Monday morning. Ask the editor if they have a minute free!

I believe that an initial approach on these lines is always best, with the possible exception of a novel that you are submitting to a publisher's slush pile. You should definitely approach on these lines if the publisher's or agent's entry in the *Writers' and Artists' Yearbook* indicates that a preliminary letter is essential. (Most agents' entries do.)

There are three pluses to this type of approach. First, you will come across (if your approach is any good) as efficient and professional. Second, you can expect a comparatively rapid response. Third, you won't waste postage (or batter your precious typescript) sending your book to somebody who is not prepared to consider it.

There's one drawback: you may feel that a very brief summary doesn't do justice to your work. How can an agent or editor judge your brilliance as a writer from a three-paragraph letter? Your exciting new theory, your subtle characterization, won't come over at all. Why should s/he take the trouble to write back and ask to see your work? Isn't it all too likely that the response – if any – will consist of a swift 'no thanks'?

I can only assure you that publishers and agents *do* write back and say 'yes please' whenever the initial approach leads them to believe that it would be worthwhile.

Often, admittedly, they do not feel it is worthwhile. But whatever the reason for this judgement, it would almost certainly apply to your complete typescript.

It you still feel dubious, however, it is perfectly acceptable to enclose a synopsis (of not more than three or four typed pages) or one sample chapter with your initial letter.

Responses to initial approaches

Initial approaches fare better if you use personal contacts than if you write to an anonymous slush pile, though you will be rejected in either case if your submission is thought unsuitable.

At literary agents Curtis Brown – one of the largest and best-known firms in the country – approximately 10 per cent of preliminary 'slush pile' submissions receive favourable replies. This adds up to around 20 submissions a week, or nearly a thousand a year. In a typical year, only four or five of these lead to Curtis Brown taking on a client and selling their book successfully.

So Curtis Brown does follow up many more submissions than they expect to accept. They ask to see every submission that they think there is any chance at all, however slight, of their accepting.

These are common reasons why the rest are rejected, all of which apply to both publishers and agents:

- *The preliminary letter is not professionally presented*. Letters must be well typed, with no mistakes, using a reasonably new ribbon. Dot matrix type is barely acceptable: the 'near letter quality' kind will do, but not the very dotty variety. They must be laid out on a sheet of white A4 (or, at a pinch, A5), bond-weight, not copy paper, in conventional business letter format. Amazingly, many would-be authors send in letters on scraps of paper torn out of notebooks, handwritten (or scrawled) in pencil or biro, full or misspellings and grammatical howlers. Their chances of acceptance are zero.

- *The preliminary letter is badly written*. Even a one- or two-paragraph letter tells an expert plenty about the author's ability to write. It must be coherent and grammatical, must put across the necessary information clearly, and should be lively – not on the 'I enclose herewith' lines. A little originality does no harm, and flashes of humour may enhance your chances, but it should not be bizarre, and must show that you can write good clear English. If you can't write a decent letter, chances are you won't write a decent book, either.

- *The subject doesn't fit the person to whom it was offered*. This doesn't necessarily imply that it has no market, just that the contact doesn't go for it. Agent Imogen Parker comments, 'An agent can only take on material if they're really personally enthusiastic about it.' The same is true of an editor.

  Nobody is interested in every subject; no novel, however accomplished, is liked by everyone who reads it. Agents and editors specialize in genres that appeal to them. You stand no chance if you've submitted a whodunnit to an agent who never touches them, or a book about sailing to somebody who finds the whole subject a dead bore. What one person thinks is an amusing letter may make another want to throw up. You may have to hunt around before you find the right home for your work.

- *The subject isn't saleable enough*. The agent or editor who reviews the submission may not be (indeed, probably isn't) an expert on the subject, but they have to make a commercial judgement on the submission. If it's for a biography of someone they have never heard of, or memoirs by someone equally unknown, or a non-fiction book on an esoteric subject where the author hasn't convinced them that there's a good market, it'll most likely be turned down.

- *The author hasn't done an adequate selling job*. Maybe they didn't come across as a pleasant, friendly, efficient individual whom anybody would be glad to deal with. Maybe their enthusiasm for the idea didn't come over – or maybe they really weren't sufficiently enthusiastic about it. Perhaps they failed to mention the right points in their letter or conversation. Whatever the reason, the author didn't make the contact eager to know more.

- *The agent or publisher isn't taking on new authors*. This is that old cliché, 'Our list is full.' Full when I apply, you may fume, but I bet they'd find room for Jeffrey Archer.

  And most likely they would. Even so, publishers generally plan to make their lists of a certain size; agents know how many clients they can comfortably handle. Some have space to spare, and some don't.

  Curtis Brown rarely turn down work for this reason: with any large agency, it's likely that at least some of the individual agents – often the newest recruits – will be taking on new clients. In a one-person literary agency, though, the solitary agent might be working flat out for existing clients, and turning away all new offers regardless of their quality.

Whatever the reason for your rejection, it is unlikely that you will be told it. Take a good hard look at your submission, polish it up if you can, and try elsewhere.

If you receive a positive reply, you will probably be asked to submit a synopsis and perhaps a sample chapter for a non-fiction book, or the complete typescript of a work of fiction.

Many literary agents also ask for a CV. Agent Imogen Parker:

> What one is looking for is to take on somebody not just for that novel but for a writing career, and so it's very important that we know more about the author than just that

they've written this book. We have to have a CV and some sort of letter which gives us an idea of what they're like, because the relationship between an agent and an author is quite close.

Striking approaches

Most slush piles are dauntingly large. Your submission, however good, will be drowned in a sea of dross. It's up to you to make it stand out, so that when a reader finally picks it up, they will be instantly attracted by it.

The best and simplest way to do this is to present it with consummate professionalism. Whether you are submitting one page or a thousand pages, it should be well typed on good quality paper, and well laid-out. (Details on how to lay out a complete typescript are given in chapter 10.)

If you have a private letterhead, use it – though there's little to be said for using your firm's letterhead. If you are planning to write professionally, you will want to invest in proper letterhead, which should be well designed (clear, striking, not too busy). It certainly isn't essential, though, for a one-book writer. Some people like to use coloured paper, though you must ensure that your letter is both legible and photocopiable.

Don't be long-winded. An initial approach is not the place to go in for long screeds about your brilliant marketing plans, or to tell your life history. All you need to do is to give your contact a first idea, so that they will be encouraged to ask for more. If and when they do ask for more, this too should be professionally presented.

Though it is inadvisable to bind a typescript, a proposal (full length, including synopsis) can look impressive if it is simply bound (again, in such a way that every page is photocopiable). Non-fiction author Suzan St Maur spiral-binds her proposals in plastic covers, starting each one with a title page on pale yellow letterhead. The effect is neat and highly professional.

A note of humour, like clear presentation and an individual style, can brighten a jaded reader's Friday afternoon. Collins' reader finds that it 'helps enormously'. But you may strike the wrong chord if you drift into whimsy.

Some authors make more dramatic efforts to stand out from the pile. George Target was working for Cassell's as an invoice clerk when he was trying to get his first novel published:

> I was filling in invoices into a book, and one day the manager said, George, nip downstairs and bring up the manuscripts. This was on a Monday morning. I went downstairs and looked in the corner of the post-room, and there were 200 impeccably typed manuscripts, absolutely perfect. And I realized for the first time in my life what I was up against. Two hundred manuscripts, sent on spec to a publisher that really wasn't interested in novels very much.
>
> That very lunchtime I went out and bought a ream of foolscap lined paper. I went home and I picked, almost at random, one of my rejected novels. I rewrote it in brown ink in italic pen, perfectly, without an error or a mistake in it. I was so neurotic, even if I made a comma wrong I'd do the whole page again. It took me about six weeks to do. Then I sent out this manuscript in quite a handsome binding. I was doing bookbinding in evening classes so I bound it up, put a coloured photograph of myself on the back.
>
> I sent it to Duckworth's. For the first time it stuck out from the mass, because it was three inches bigger than anyone else's, and when it was opened it was in impeccable, beautiful Renaissance italic. So for the first time, I believe, it was read.

It was also accepted. I hesitate to recommend the handwritten approach to today's hopefuls, but the underlying philosophy was sound.

Target has tried various other methods to impress editors with his eccentric personality:

> I used to write for women's magazines under various pseudonyms and I used to stick little photographs of my children – without comment – on the front cover. Or I would take a little scent spray and just give it a little whiff on the inside cover, so when they opened it, instead of the dreary smell of coffee, they would at least have Chanel No. 5 or something.

I used to address people by strange names. One editor accepted a story of mine just before Christmas. I was so pleased I called her 'Sister Christmas' and I've called her that ever since. I've got a relationship with this lady. Every time she writes me a letter she sticks a little Christmas picture on, or plastic holly. Though she's bought little of my work since, at least I've got a working relationship with a human being who thinks, who is this madman up in Norfolk?

Multiple submissions

The classic rule for authors used to be, submit your manuscript to one agent or publisher at a time. The argument for this was (and still is) that any agent or publisher might justifiably be annoyed if they had spent all weekend reading your work, only to find on Monday morning that you had already sold it to someone else. It was also the only practicable approach for most writers in the days before word processors and photocopiers.

But the one-at-a-time approach can be extremely time-consuming when agents and editors take months to reply (as they generally do), and the likelihood of two publishers coming back to say 'yes' on the same day is not high. It's understandable that many authors should have begun to question this system, particularly now that they can cheaply and easily produce multiple copies of their work.

It is now considered acceptable for agents to send out multiple submissions (that is, to offer work to several publishers simultaneously) and there is no reason why unrepresented authors should not copy them.

If you do send out multiple submissions, you should make it clear that you are doing so. You may feel that this will prejudice your chances of being seriously considered, and that the odds of being found out and punished if you don't say are low. Even so, my advice is to own up. This could even be to your advantage. Patrick Janson-Smith of Transworld:

I think it shows great initiative. It would create a sense of excitement. Actually, a multiple submission – if an author wrote to me out of the blue and said, this is on offer to So-and-so, So-and-so, So-and-so, I might take it possibly a little bit more seriously.

Because a lot of submissions come and there's no pressure on the publisher, he tends to say, I'll look at that one there because I've got to get back to Heinemann because there's an auction [i.e., where a number of publishers bid for the same rights] on the fourteenth or whatever. I find a back-by date very useful as a discipline.

There is one drawback. Even if your rejection notes are brief and uninformative, rejections can lead you to take a more critical view of your work, and to revise and improve it before re-offering it. If you send a submission that isn't quite up to standard – but could be made so with a rethink – to several publishers simultaneously, then you may suffer several simultaneous rejections, and be stumped for a publisher to offer it to after you've re-honed it.

Waiting for a verdict

Publishers and agents can take for ever even to look at short initial letters. There is no reason why an author should wait for ever, and if a publisher holds on to your proposal for six months without acknowledging it, you might justifiably conclude that they are a chronically inefficient firm by whom you would not want to be published in any case.

Ideally, every firm should acknowledge receipt of proposals by return of post. Most do not. If you are anxious to be reassured that your typescript has been received safely, then include your own acknowledgement (on a stamped, addressed postcard) with it. Any passably efficient firm should manage to pop this into the 'out' tray without delay.

You cannot expect a verdict by return of post – and agents and publishers rarely give them, because when they do, many authors promptly grumble that their submission can't have been considered carefully enough. Two months is a realistic time to wait for a response to an initial letter; allow three months for a full typescript.

If you have heard nothing at the end of this period, it makes sense to chase the publisher or agent by phone or letter.

How long you wait subsequently, before requesting the typescript back or submitting the proposal to another firm or both, is entirely up to you. Pressing hard might move your submission to the top of the pile; alternatively, the publisher or agent might be prompted to ship it back to you unread. It will also depend upon factors such as the number of alternative publishers you have on your list, and the number of rejections you have already suffered.

If a publisher indicates that they have looked at your submission and have a serious interest in publishing your book, you will need to allow them time to explore the possibility of publishing it successfully. This may involve sending your submission to one or two experts in your field, for their comments on its contents and approach; trying out the idea on sales people; calculating costings; an editor submitting the proposition to the Board for approval. When pushed (for instance, by a deadline for a book auction), publishers manage to do these things very rapidly; when not under pressure, they regularly use them to justify further months of delay. This does not mean, however, that you should automatically disbelieve an editor who makes excuses. He or she may genuinely be making great efforts to convince colleagues that your book should be accepted.

So a long delay can be a hopeful sign, and can lead to acceptance. Judith Lennox-Smith sent the typescript of her novel *Reynardine* to Hamish Hamilton (via the slush pile) in December 1986. She heard nothing for four months, after which she wrote to ask what had happened to it. Hamish Hamilton subsequently came back to her to say that they were seriously interested, but wanted her to make some changes. The novel was eventually accepted – after revision – in January 1988, and published a year later.

Not all delays are eventually resolved by success, however. A publisher is not committed to publishing your book until you and they sign a contract. Sometimes publishers string authors along, expressing serious interest for a year or even two years, then finally reject the submission. Novelist George Target:

> I show my writing class all the delaying letters. I showed them one yesterday from Ashford Press. "I know we've been rather a long time making up our minds" – that's

since last March! Ten months! – ''but if you can hang on to just after Christmas . . .''

This kind of delay doesn't lead any writer to conclude that the publisher is eager to publish their work. Most likely it's a borderline decision whether or not to take it, and this may mean that the book, if bought, will not be promoted with any great enthusiasm. Unless you've suffered repeated disappointments elsewhere, this may be the stage at which you choose to warn the publishers that unless they come up with a firm offer within a fortnight, you will offer the book to someone else. Perhaps the next publisher you try will like it better – and be more efficient, too.

CHAPTER 5

Synopses and submissions

If the publisher or agent to whom you sent your initial letter replies favourably, s/he will next ask you for a longer submission.

With a novel, autobiography, memoirs or anything similar, this may consist of the complete typescript. It can be helpful also to enclose a synopsis to give the reader an overview of the plot. Alternatively, if the typescript is very long, you might at this stage submit a synopsis and perhaps three sample chapters.

For any other type of non-fiction book, the submission will be centred on a synopsis.

It's almost certain that at some point before your book is published, you will need to provide a synopsis. There's much to be said for preparing one *before* you write the book. Then you can use it as a template to help you organize your writing.

The pros and cons of writing to a synopsis

If you are a non-fiction author, writing a tightly-organized book on a very factual subject, there is everything to be said for using a synopsis. These are the obvious advantages:

- *It is (as I've already explained) your primary selling tool.*
- *It helps you (and your editor or agent) to judge whether your idea is meaty enough to make an entire book.* Even with practice, it isn't easy to judge how many words you will be able to write about something. For the inex-

perienced it's often extremely difficult. It will help nobody if you agree to write a book on a specialist subject, then find you've run out of things to say on page 10. A synopsis will reassure you and your editor that there is a book's worth in your idea; conversely, it could help you expand or narrow your idea to a reasonable book span.

Of course, it's not true that there are a fixed number of words that can be written on any subject. Some skilful writers can spin out the flimsiest topic for page after page. Others have a naturally concise style, and would exhaust the same material in half a page or less. Only experience can teach you how your own writing style relates to a synopsis, and how much material you can fit into (or need in order to fill) a page, a chapter, a book.

- *It helps you and your editor or agent to agree what topics you will cover*. It's at the synopsis stage that the editor or agent may point out a major aspect of the subject that s/he thinks should be covered but that you hadn't planned to include.

  It's a common failing of amateur non-fiction writers to include only topics that they know well, and to omit aspects of their subject that would be of equal interest to their readers, but that are not as familiar to them. If you want to be published, you must tailor your book to suit your readers. If you don't know something that readers would expect to learn from a book on your proposed subject, it's your job to find it out.

  Most likely your editor or agent will not be an expert in your specialist subject, and will not be in the best possible position to judge the adequacy of your proposed contents. To overcome this difficulty, publishers (and sometimes agents) frequently send submissions to outside experts for comment.

- *It helps you and your editor to agree what weight should be given to different topics*. You need to ensure that you assign plenty of space for what you consider to be vital issues, and less space to peripheral matters. You also need to ensure that you and your editor (or the expert) agree which issues *are* vital. If you plan to give lots of space to a pet theory, and this won't be acceptable to the publishers, it's best to resolve the disagreement at this early stage.

- *It helps you to plan your coverage.* You make sure everything will fit in somewhere. You ensure that there's no unnecessary repetition, that the order flows logically, that there's a sensible beginning and end. In order to organize the presentation of a complex subject in the best possible way, it's necessary to plan in advance. Some people are good at doing this in their heads, and don't have a vital need to write it all down. But in that case it's no big deal for them to regurgitate the contents of their heads onto paper.
- *It helps you to pace yourself.* Your publisher will tell you how long s/he wants your book to be. Your job is to ensure that you cover all the necessary points within that span. If you're writing about crossing the Gobi Desert, you don't want to get to the end of your word allowance and find you are still only two miles in.
- *It makes the writing seem less daunting.* Non-fiction writer Suzan St Maur:

> It makes the whole project far less terrifying for the novice, as it's more digestible to think of the book in terms of, let's say, twelve projects of 5,000 words rather than one of 60,000.

The major argument against using a synopsis is that it can be difficult to keep to it when actually writing the book. You may carry out much of your research after your synopsis has been agreed, and what you discover may lead you to rethink your subject, or the best way of presenting it. You may find that a topic that you thought would make ten pages can adequately be covered in one, or vice versa.

Publishers do appreciate this, and they do not generally insist that a writer keeps very closely to his or her synopsis, unless there is a very good reason (for example, the book is highly illustrated and tightly laid out, and deviation would cause knock-on problems to the illustrator, picture researcher and designer). Naturally they will not be impressed if they requested changes to your original conception, and you subsequently prove not to have taken them on board.

Jasper Ridley, historical biographer:

> I make the synopsis in my head, and the whole book is there. But when I have to do a synopsis for a publisher I have to do it at an earlier stage of course, before I've started on the research. That's why I very often vary from that synopsis, because I change my mind in the course of the research.

Writing fiction to a synopsis

Many novelists also use synopses as working tools. Historical novelist Pat Barr:

> I do write synopses, though I vary from them a little bit. I've always been interested and amazed by authors who say they get one idea and two characters and the thing takes off from there. It doesn't work for me, there's no doubt about that. I have to more or less follow through a rough story line and develop the characters before I start.

Frederick Forsyth, who researches and prepares his books meticulously before he writes them very rapidly (in less than two months), writes out a long synopsis, usually of about a tenth of the finished book length, which he uses as a working guide and also submits to his publishers.

George Target thinks his ideas through before he begins to write, but he likes to keep them in his head:

> When you come down to it, there's this old, old bit that many writers try and kid you with, that the characters take over and they try to hear the voices speaking. I don't accept that at all. I am in charge of what I write, and so I know by the first couple of days how it is going to go. I wish I could get it all down on paper in a couple of days, because I find the two months that I spend writing it down dead boring, because I know what's going to happen.
>
> I would find a synopsis rather deadening. You think, oh my God, I've got to find 2,000 words to fit *that* paragraph. Keeping it in my mind, though I know where it's going to go, the details can alter.

Romance writer Elizabeth Oldfield plots by chapter. Her Mills & Boon romances generally contain eight or nine chapters, so she works out the story in this format, and then aims to write a chapter a week. She rarely starts any story and then abandons it. This low reject rate is common among successful novelists. Kathy Page:

> I have lots of ideas that I write down, but literally just as a sentence. Novel about X. And then they just never recur to me, and I never look through the notebook again, so those obviously haven't got enough behind them. But once I start writing a chapter, then I've never not finished.

Other writers take a more uncertain approach. Jeremy Leland:

> I may only have a distant idea of what I'm aiming at, but there is always a particular image that I am pursuing.

Cynthia Harrod-Eagles, historical novelist:

> I usually have a rough idea of how things are going to go when I start, but I find if I plot it in too much detail to begin with, I lose interest in writing it. Part of the reason that I write is in order to find out what happens, because it never works out the way that it starts off.

Such an approach avoids the deadening effect of a synopsis that George Target complains of, but it can lead to a high failure rate. Writers' block in mid-novel is much more likely if you don't know what's going to happen next, than if you do. M. E. Austen is another intuitive novelist who begins with a general image, but no clear idea of how his plot is going to be resolved. Writing his first novel, *Love-Act*, he found this approach very successful, but he has since discovered some of the drawbacks. None of his four subsequent novels have been published.

Austen admits that his brainstorming style is inefficient: he spends a lot of time exploring blind alleys. He not only revises heavily, he abandons many scenes entirely. He feels in retrospect that his second novel was too ambitious in scope, and the third, though it started well, 'ran out of steam' in its second half. His problem is compounded by the fact that he isn't a writer who thrives on revision. He finds that he writes best when he manages to write quickly. Passages that he labours over never achieve the same quality. Though he has doubts about changing his working style, it's evident that his current practice doesn't always serve him well.

Using a synopsis to sell fiction

Frederick Forsyth believes it was his 20-page synopsis of *The Day of the Jackal* that swung the odds in favour of getting this, his first book, published. He received four rejections when he tried to sell the book on the basis of a complete typescript. Then he wrote the synopsis, offered this and not the typescript to the next publisher - and it was promptly accepted. As Forsyth points out, this is largely because *The Day of the Jackal* is a book that looks good in a synopsis. Reading the first few pages of the book, it's understandable that editors might not be impressed. Is this a novel about the assassination of General de Gaulle? Everybody knows that General de Gaulle wasn't assassinated. It probably struck them as rather silly. From the synopsis, however, it's evident that the book is very ingeniously plotted, and its appeal is much more obvious.

Agent Imogen Parker, who handles largely 'literary' fiction, takes an opposite view:

> I'm not really all that interested in people's synopses for novels. I'm interested in the way they write, though obviously if there are flaws in the plot one would have to point that out.

Arguably this is because for Parker's type of novel, the overall plot is less important than the style. Often relatively little actually happens in a literary novel: it's much less easy to convey its quality through the medium of a synopsis. Even a very good synopsis rarely does much to compensate for a slow start to a book. Book buyers won't see your full synopsis, only a few paragraphs of blurb on the cover. And if the editor is thinking wearily, 'Does anything original or anything at all ever happen in this book?' s/he will scarcely be reassured by a synopsis that proves that no, nothing ever *does* happen.

It's largely for your own benefit that a synopsis proves useful. Even if you didn't originally write to a synopsis, there's much to be said for writing one after you've completed a draft of your novel. Flaws in the plot that weren't apparent to you from close up may be glaringly evident when you try to summarize it. Even if your novel relies more upon mood and character than upon a conventional story, it's a useful exercise to try to summarize what it's about in a couple of pages. The authors of successful novels are generally very clear what they are trying to say in them, in terms of underlying theme as well as plot. Unsuccessful novelists sometimes give the impression that they are not.

Whatever post-structuralist critics claim, it's rare that anybody finds a theme, a recurring image or any other literary effect in a novel without the author consciously putting it there in the first place. George Target:

> If I write in an effect it's a deliberate effect. I don't believe there can be unexpected effects.

Except, that is, for unwanted and unsuccessful ones.

Setting out a synopsis

There's no firm rule about how long a synopsis should be, how it should be set out, or what it should contain. All of these can vary greatly according to the type of book. A synopsis for a biography will be quite different from the synopsis for a school textbook, and both will differ from that for a cookery book.

If the book is to be written in chapters, it's normal to adopt a chapter structure for the synopsis. A paragraph to each chapter is a typical length: say, two to three pages of single-spaced A4 to describe an average-length book. If the book is to be tightly structured with lots of sections and sub-sections, a list of sub-section titles might make an adequate synopsis.

Though this length of synopsis is generally sufficient to win a contract for a non-fiction book, it's a good idea to write a much more detailed synopsis when the research is completed, and before the text is written. This isn't for the publisher, it's primarily for you, though you may (like Frederick Forsyth) also choose to show it to your publisher. Some writers prepare this kind of detailed synopsis for the whole book before they begin to write a word, while others work chapter by chapter. Biographer Michael Holroyd's working method is a good example:

> Biography isn't just information retrieval; non-fiction isn't simply an accumulation of facts. There are sometimes legitimate ways of escaping the prison of chronology. They have to be legitimate. Sometimes I have ideas of getting away from chronology which don't work. But in Shaw's case [Bernard Shaw, Holroyd's most recent subject] it's not a simple chronological work because he had such a protean life, with so many careers within it. I have to follow one line and stop it at a natural break and pursue another line also to a natural break, which may not be exactly the same date.
>
> So it's built up like a wall of bricks which don't all come to end at the same place. That is a very complicated structure, but I hope it doesn't read as if it's complicated, I hope it reads perfectly naturally . . .
>
> I plan a chapter structure in no great detail, but I do plan it. It's speculative. I say, probably there will be five sections, I'll deal with this, that and then the other thing. So I do have a piece of paper, quite a small piece of paper, on which the general structure is foretold . . .
>
> Then having done that I say, what flows into what? How shall I begin and end? I know what I'm dealing with, but what is the evolution and development of this section? I then programme it in more detail, assembling a mass of small connections with echoes from the past and prophesies of the future. This is the texture of the narrative.
>
> Sometimes I will find that it doesn't work, that I have made all these connections and at the end of it, there's something which should have been in there that I haven't been able to fit in. I haven't been able to find a place for it. Then I may have to reassemble everything. Or I may say, the reason why I left that out is that really when I think of it, it's not important.
>
> Or sometimes I will say, no, that was the wrong set of connections, it should be the other way round, because the reason why that's not in is that there has been a false connection, and so I have to redo it. So there's quite detailed planning about the whole chapter, which may change

quite a lot in the process of writing, though it will cover approximately the same area.

There's a slight tendency for me to cover less than I believe I will, and to postpone something for later on where I like to think I see a better place for it. But that's always dangerous, because if I have too much waiting for me, either I will forget it, or I find that things become congested later.

Other elements of a submission

Your submission should not consist only of a chapter-by-chapter (or similar) synopsis. You need to put together a well-arranged package which will do the most effective job possible of selling your book to the publisher or agent. For a non-fiction book it should contain, in a sensible order, most or all of these elements:

- *Your name, the working title, and (unless the title makes this absolutely clear) a very brief description of the book*. For example:

How to Write a Book and Get it Published
A complete guide to the publishing maze by Susan Curran

or:

The Ape Clog
A biography of William de la Pole, 1st Duke of Suffolk
A proposal for a new book by Susan Curran

Some authors suggest alternative titles, in case the editor doesn't like their original title.

- *An introduction*. A paragraph or two of blurb, to give an impression of the kind of book you plan to write, and bring to the fore any particular reasons you have for wanting to write it. For example:

A popular guide to writing books and getting them published, covering both fiction and non-fiction. It takes the reader through every stage from developing an initial idea, to research and writing and eventually finding a publisher and negotiating the contract. The emphasis is on practical advice and information.

or:

William de la Pole, Earl (later Duke) of Suffolk (1396–1450) fought in Agincourt, was defeated at Orleans by Joan of Arc, and later became a minister of King Henry VI. He was the major power behind Henry's reign from 1447 until 1450, when he was impeached, exiled, captured at sea by pirates on his way to France, and beheaded. This will be the first full-length modern biography of an outstanding medieval soldier, statesman and poet.

- *A note on the market for your book*. Indicate who you expect to buy your book. If you have an idea how many potential buyers there are, indicate this too. For example:

It is estimated that 300,000 homes in the UK now own an X-type widget. This how-to-use-it manual should be a must for all X-type owners.

or:

Forty thousand people in the UK belong to model railways clubs. I have authorized access to the mailing list for the Northern England Modellers, a club with 10,000 members.

or:

This book should appeal to MBA students, students of business studies in polytechnics and universities, and be of some value to A-level Economics students. It follows the syllabus of (name of qualification) and I hope it will become a set book on many business studies courses.

The publisher may take any sales estimate you offer with a large pinch of salt, but solid information like this is very useful to them.

- *A brief comment on the competition*. If your proposed book will be in direct competition with an existing title (particularly a big-selling title), acknowlege that – and go on to explain how your book will differ from (and be better than) its rival.
- *Suggested length and format*. Indicate how long you

envisage making your book, and whether you would be prepared to adapt this length to meet a publisher's requirements. If you have a clear idea of the format you want (size, layout, number of illustrations) then indicate it. However, it's not wise to be too insistent on details at this early stage.

If you intend to supply illustrations (or if the book requires, or would benefit from, illustrations that you cannot supply), give brief details.

- *Your qualifications as author*. A brief CV (minimum one paragraph; maximum, say, one page) which emphasizes your qualifications for writing and promoting this book. For example:

> I have been a model railway enthusiast for thirty years, and am currently treasurer of the Northern England Modellers. For the last five years I have written a regular column in *Modellers Monthly*.
>
> The book will be based on my PhD thesis on the Duke of Suffolk (degree granted by Blankshire University in 19XX), but will be extensively rewritten for a general audience.

Follow this with your synopsis of the proposed contents. A fiction synopsis will contain less general material. A general résumé of the plot (there's no need to break it down into chapters, though you may find it helpful to do so), and a comment on yourself as author, is sufficient. For example:

> Mary Bloggs is the author of twelve previous novels, including *The Chronicles of Blankshire* which won the XXX Prize in 19XX.

Setting out a submission

It's best to set out your submission as a self-contained whole, and send it with a separate covering letter. The submission can then be detached from the letter, and photocopied for sending to an outside expert whose opinion is needed; or from an agent to a publisher; or from a junior editor to a more senior editor within the same company.

Don't crowd it. An extra sheet of paper doesn't cost much.

Set it out as attractively as possible. Leave plenty of white space, include clear headings, and avoid large unbroken chunks of text. Start each new section of more than a paragraph's length on a separate sheet. Number each sheet, and head each sheet with your name and the working title of the book, abbreviated if necessary.

It will, of course, all be neatly typed. It's not essential to double space. Some people prefer to, while others prefer it single-spaced. Though full typescripts should consist of loose pages, short submissions can be stapled together or simply bound.

Protecting your ideas

It isn't necessary for you to mark either your typescript or your short submission with a copyright notice. Except in the USA, you automatically acquire copyright in everything original you write: there's no formal registration process.

There's no copyright in ideas, however, only in the words in which they are expressed. So there is nothing in law to prevent somebody from stealing your brilliantly original idea for a thriller, and writing the story up in their own words. (It would, however, count as plagiarism if you wrote up in your own words a story that closely imitated the plot of a published book such as *The Day of the Jackal*.)

Some authors do worry that publishers may steal their ideas. It's possible, although publishers regularly retort that the only authors who worry about this are those whose ideas have little merit in the first place. It certainly isn't the normal practice of reputable publishers and agents to lift one writer's idea and pass it on to some other writer. Sometimes, though, it may be clear that while you have a brilliant idea, you simply don't have the writing skill to do justice to it. In that case the publisher or agent might possibly ask your permission to offer it to somebody else, or s/he might advise you to enlist the help of a co-author or ghostwriter. You have every right to ask for payment (though it may not be as substantial as you might hope) if this happens.

Large publishers receive thousands of submissions each year, and it's also possible for the same publisher to be offered an *X-type Widget Book* by two different authors. Perhaps yours was the first submission; perhaps it was, unknown to you, the second, third or subsequent submission. Perhaps two similar proposals went to two different editors. If the other submission won the contract, it might look unfair to you, but it wouldn't really be unfair, and you would have no reason to expect compensation.

A small minority of authors complain bitterly in these circumstances, and a smaller minority try to take legal action. It rarely if ever benefits them to do so. An idea, however brilliant, is only a small part of a book. It's naturally annoying if you find that you can't make use of your idea, for whatever reason. But that's a poor reason for not promoting your ideas in the first place. Your best bet is to forget the incident, and work on developing a new idea.

CHAPTER 6
Research and preparation

Mills & Boon editors did a double-take when they were offered a romance that featured tigers in the Australian Bush. Original, but perhaps a little too fantastical for their market? Agent Imogen Parker wasn't too impressed, either, by the novelist who mentioned that well-known dual carriageway, Haverstock Hill. She knows Haverstock Hill; the author evidently didn't.

The oldest and most basic advice to writers is that they should write about what they know, but most of us don't even know our own street well enough to write about it without going outside to check the odd detail – and most of us need to move beyond the end of our street in order to write something interesting. Whether you have a lifetime's experience of your subject matter, or you invented a space city setting five minutes ago, you need to research and prepare before you begin to write your book.

Good research can make a book; bad research, or no research, wrecks it. Whether you are writing a contemporary novel or an academic reference work, your research will probably take at least as long as (and maybe several times longer than) your writing.

It's important to approach your research as systematically as possible, particularly if you will need to travel long distances or to interview people. It's no good realizing after you've returned home from that library in Washington that you didn't copy the vital paragraph of a letter. Courtesy demands that you don't repeatedly pester interviewees by ringing up or calling again to check on facts that you could and should have got straight the first time.

It's also important to start by devising a filing system that will not only cope with all the material for this book, but will still be functioning adequately when you're writing your fifteenth book. I can only give a brief introduction here to a complex subject. It would benefit almost every writer to read Ann Hoffmann's invaluable and very complete guide, *Research for Writers* (see Bibliography).

Sources of information

They vary almost infinitely. Your own experience; the experience of others, gleaned through letters, questionnaires, phone calls and face-to-face interviews; material in books, magazines and newspapers; geographical information gleaned from visiting locations that will feature in your book; all have a part to play.

Don't overlook the simplest sources. There's no need to trek to a city library to consult a book if there's a copy in your local library. A lending library wins out over a reference library, a library with open shelves over one with closed stacks, if the same book is obtainable from both. Most libraries – including university libraries – will provide reference access to bona fide researchers, and many will allow you to borrow books if you make a formal written request. It's as well to write to, or phone, the librarian before making a long journey, particularly if you want to consult material that is not on open access. Otherwise you may waste precious hours waiting while it is retrieved from store for you.

Consulting library books costs you – in travelling time and in train or bus fares, or petrol and car park fees. If you will need to refer to a book constantly, you may find it more economical, as well as more convenient, to buy a copy. You will also need to build up your own reference library, including (but not limited to) a good general dictionary, specialist dictionaries (foreign dictionaries, dictionaries of phrases and quotations, subject dictionaries), a thesaurus, a road atlas, a world atlas, and the *Writers' and Artists' Yearbook* or *The Writer's Handbook*.

Interviewing people

Many people are genuinely pleased to help writers, by talking to them at length, providing access to private papers, and letting them explore private property. It never hurts to ask - even the busiest and most eminent may well find time for you. But do remember that other people's time is valuable, and try to use it economically.

Try not to demand lengthy interviews before you have reasonable assurance that your book will be published. Don't ask people to tell you things that you could readily discover from books or journals. Don't expect them to do your research for you: if neither you nor they have the answer to a question readily to hand, it's your job to locate it, not theirs.

Prepare your questions thoroughly. Never take co-operation for granted: remember your interviewee is doing you a favour. If you prefer tape interviews, ask permission before switching on your tape recorder. Write to thank interviewees afterwards, and if they have made a substantial contribution to your book, ask them how they would like their help to be acknowledged in it. (Send them a copy when it is published, too.)

If you plan to use direct quotes - as I have in this book - then ensure that you have the interviewee's permission to do so. I suggest that you offer to let your interviewee review the quotes you plan to use. Journalists do not normally do this, but you are not a journalist: you will be working to a longer time-scale, and it's to your advantage to stay on good terms with your informants. Nothing sours relations faster than quoting somebody saying something they wish they hadn't said, even if your quote is accurate and in context.

It is not usual to pay interviewees, or to pay for the use of quotes from interviews.

The situation is different if you wish to quote from private papers. All written material, published or unpublished, is copyright, and you must obtain the written permission of the copyright holder (who will not necessarily be the owner of the paper) before quoting from or paraphrasing it. (There are some minor exceptions, which are explained in some detail in the *Writers' and Artists' Yearbook*.)

Fees requested for permission to quote vary from zero to quite substantial sums, even for small excerpts. It is not uncommon for permission to be refused, as might well be done, for example, if you are writing an unauthorized biography and an authorized biography of the same person is planned.

Writing about what you know

Not only does this save you research, it generally works better than if you try to write about something you know little or nothing about.

Romantic novelist Clare Lavenham has worked all her life as a hospital librarian. Hers must be among the very few books which regularly feature hospital librarians as heroines. She specializes in doctor and nurse romances, which work well, she feels, because she understands what life in a hospital is like. She has enough specialist knowledge to use medical terms accurately on the relatively simple level demanded by a romance plot, and if she needs more information she is in a perfect position to research it, by consulting books or by asking colleagues.

Pat Barr writes historical novels set in the Far East: an exotic subject, but again one that is based on personal experience. She has lived in Japan and travelled widely in the East; she has written a series of non-fiction books about Westerners living and travelling in the East. This is the subject with which she feels comfortable: in contrast, she says, 'I don't think I could ever write a modern novel, at least not set in England.'

Barr is also careful to recognize her limitations. She focuses on Western characters in the East, rather than on orientals:

> I can't totally do a leap into another racial head, though I came closest to it in *Kenjiro*, where one of the main characters is a Japanese man. But although they may be important to the story, I very rarely even make the attempt to get inside foreigners' heads very much, because I think that I really don't know enough to do that.

Would-be writers often make the mistake of over-estimating the accuracy and completeness of what they have learned at second-hand. If you want to write a spy story, it really isn't sufficient to have read lots of other people's spy stories, or to have watched a few spy dramas on television. If you haven't been a spy yourself, you need to do very thorough first-hand research: talking to current or former spies and reading non-fiction books about spying, as well as researching your locations and props (the gun he pulls out, the atomic research station he bugs) comprehensively.

Similarly, it's a bad idea to set a romance in an office unless you have worked in an office. You may think you know what goes on in offices, but a reader who works in one will probably realize on the first page that you don't understand all the minutiae of the daily routine.

One obvious drawback is that you may feel your own life and environs provide insufficiently enthralling material. Possibly you misjudge them. Many English would-be romance writers try setting their stories in the Australian outback; readers from the Australian outback regularly write to Mills & Boon to complain not only that the Australian outback is not remotely as they imagine it (even disallowing the shortage of stunningly handsome, eligible men), but that they would much rather read more stories set in Scotland. Your childhood in the suburbs of Birmingham may seem as exotic to a reader in the USA as a childhood in New Orleans or Santa Fé would seem to you.

An alternative way of getting round the credibility problem is to write about something that will not be any more familiar to any of your readers than it is to you – most obviously by writing sheer fantasy, or setting your story in the past or future. I chose to write historical novels myself largely because I wanted to explore political themes which I felt I could not handle credibly in a contemporary novel. After thorough research, however, I feel I've made as good an attempt to recreate the atmosphere and intrigue of fifteenth-century politics as is possible from a twentieth-century standpoint.

How writers organize their research

Most writers confess to being less well organized than they would ideally like to be, and I have yet to encounter a writer who handles much of their research by computer. Often this is for the basic practical reason that research information comes in many different forms – photocopies, press cuttings, notes taken down in libraries, photographs – and it would not be a realistic proposition to make it all computer-readable.

Some writers manage to handle the most astonishing volumes of information. Juri Gabriel compiled a world camping guide which involved collating between 15 and 20 *thousand* questionnaires about campsites. He reckoned he had to 'keep up to 160,000 bits of paper in the air at once' – and he didn't use a computer. The trick, he found, was to enlist out of work PhDs as his researchers: they proved much more efficient than the less well qualified.

Writers face two problems: what to research, and how to retrieve the information when they need it. Cynthia Harrod-Eagles, prolific historical novelist whose *Dynasty* series spans several centuries:

> First of all I read the general histories of the period, to get a rough idea of the shape of things, than usually I go to the bibliography to find out what their sources were. Eventually you get back to the one or two who seem to be the authorities on the period, and from there you can see how they attained their authority. And if it looks a bit questionable, which it often is, then you can go back and look at the original documents. All that's less important once you get more up to date.
>
> When I started with the fifteenth century you really had to go back to original documents because there was just so little written. But now I'm at the beginning of the nineteenth century the sources are all pretty well verified, so you can be sure of them.
>
> Then of course you have to look into specialist branches of information which won't be covered by general histories. The last book I did covered the battle of Trafalgar, so I had to look up the history of the navy, and various books on sailing and shipbuilding and the commission structure and what sailors ate and how they were paid. Then I looked up the details of the actual campaigns, which were all in separate books.
>
> Then I consulted books on costume, books on furniture, books on artefacts of all kinds. I needed to know about Factory Acts, and farming, and coal mining, and herbalism, and gardening – it just goes on and on and on. There are so

many specialist branches, and of course you might be writing one fairly unimportant incident in a chapter, and you suddenly realize you don't know what herb they would have clapped on this wound. And you might go off on a two-day chase trying to find out this one single piece of information.

I have everything written out on pieces of paper – quite large pieces of paper – and what I can keep in a book I won't bother to copy out in any form, because I usually remember where I got it from in the first place. But if it's something that I've got to extract from a book I usually put it on a very large sheet of paper which will be kept in a file under fairly rough headings. I've got a file for cotton manufacture, and I've got a file for horses and carriages, because I use those a lot. They're just pocket files, and I put the little papers in loose.

All this is done in order to write fiction: when writing non-fiction the research has to be even more exhaustive. Michael Holroyd, who specializes in biographies of writers and artists:

I read the published work. I read books on surrounding matter, just to get my terms of reference, to know the man. Then I fill in the detail by going to unpublished works, which can be all over the world, either privately held or in public institutions.

When I see a letter, or some diaries, or other manuscripts, I have to decide, Do I want the whole of this? – in which case perhaps I can have a photocopy. Do I want two sentences? Why do I want them? How will I catalogue this? Is it something by date? Is it something about a play or a book? Is it something about a subject? Is it just an example of humour, politics, human nature? How on earth am I going to file it so that when I need the information I can retrieve it?

You mustn't take too much from libraries, or else you inundate yourself. On the other hand you don't want to think, my God, I now remember that letter I read in Texas, I must now go back and get it.

In libraries I work very hard because I am constantly having to make decisions. What do I really need? Sometimes a single letter can give me something about the work, something that is relevant to what happened in the life at that date, and something on a completely different subject, so there may be three sentences you take out and file in different places.

I keep an alphabetical list of manuscript material. I keep some form of chronology, and I file things also under title, itinerary and under subject. I try to cross-reference, but not always successfully.

Contemporary research has to be just as exhaustive. Frederick Forsyth, for example, takes about six months to research each of his books. He begins as soon as he has the storyline roughed out. By making all his props – he describes real weapons, real planes and so on in detail – his characters' procedures and his locations totally authentic, he argues, he can give credibility to any plot so long as it is feasible.

Forsyth likes to research by talking to experts. If he wants to feature a jumbo jet, for instance, he'll contact a pilots' association and ask to be introduced to a pilot who can tell him about jumbo jets. His journalist's background stands him in good stead here. Even when he is dealing with sensitive topics, he reckons he can normally find out what he wants to know eventually. His note taking is, he claims, fairly haphazard. And when it comes to filing and retrieval, 'everything gets dropped into the box file'.

Any competent author reckons to know far more about their subject than they will actually include in the book. That fascinating detail about flight control most likely won't be mentioned in the final draft: indeed it's proabably better not mentioned, or it may clutter your narrative. It will have served its purpose if knowing it gives you confidence while you are writing, and frees you so that you don't have to let what you know, rather than what you want to say, shape your story.

The same is true of non-fiction books. John Hedgecoe, photographer and writer:

I do a lot of work beforehand. I might have travelled on two or three trips abroad – to the Far East, Middle East, Scandinavia or somewhere – and shot a lot of pictures. We might use 4 or 500 pictures, but I might have many thousands to choose from. Generally I could alter the contents 100 per cent or even 300 per cent. I've got millions of

> pictures in my files, but I'm a terrible filer, so I prefer to shoot new pictures.

So many authors confess to being terrible filers. However, the other alternative – of becoming so wrapped up in a complex cross-referencing system that you never progress beyond it to the writing – is perhaps even worse.

A card index filed alphabetically by subject – either with full information on the subject written on each card, or with cross-references to places where the information is to be found – is perhaps the most reliable filing system, but many very professional authors use quite different methods. Jasper Ridley, historical biographer:

> I take my notes in little notebooks which I put in my pocket. I'm always afraid that I'm going to lose my notes – as a friend of mine once did – and I feel these notebooks, which I put in my pocket, are quite safe.
>
> For John Knox I filled about 200 of these notebooks, and for Henry VIII I think about 130. Writing about Garibaldi I brought back more information on photocopies.
>
> I go through the letters taking notes, and the letters in each collection are usually in more or less chronological order. Occasionally they're not, and I make notes that are also out of order. If I'm in a hurry to find something in my notes this can be a problem.
>
> I check my facts when compiling my footnotes, and sometimes I simply cannot find a reference to something. I may have to spend four or five days looking for it, and sometimes I reluctantly come to the conclusion I have imagined it. That's very easy to do. You read a report of a conversation and without realizing it you imagine what you think he said next and you put it in.
>
> When I was writing about John Knox, I started making an index to my notes. I found it took me seven or eight months to do this, and I think it would take longer to make the index than to try and find my way without the index.

Fictional elements

It's not only the real locations, incidents and props of a book that need to be convincing. In a novel, it's also necessary to convince your readers of the reality of your fictional settings and characters.

Many writers go to great lengths to do this. George Target:

> I wrote a novel called *The Americans*, which was about a whole town outside an RAF base. There are 400 named characters, and I had that all ready before I wrote a word. I was marching through the town, I was going to the record shop, to the grocery shop, attending church, going out to the airbase. I knew that town backwards.

Target likes drawing maps of his fictional locations. He is currently writing a novel about a small village. He has taken an Ordnance Survey map of the general area where his fictional village is located, cut it in half, and taped a sheet of blank paper in between the two halves. On that, he has extended the real roads so that they lead to his imaginary village, and planned it all out in Ordnance Survey fashion.

It's just as important to visualize your characters' houses, schools and offices. Can Bill in the dining room see Mary in the kitchen? Going from Fred's office to Jim's office, do you pass Jane's office? As the creator of these places, you need to know. You need to be consistent from scene to scene, so that your readers too can visualize these places successfully. It helps if you plan out every recurring location – by sketching out the layout, or even making a model – before you begin to write. Then you won't need to interrupt the flow of your writing to consider the logistics of your scene.

The more you know about your characters, the more real they will seem to you when you write about them, and to your readers when they read about them. Again, you need to know far more than you mention in the course of the story. It's advisable to work out a full biography and description of each major character, again before you begin to write.

You don't have to write this down, but it will help if you do, if only in ensuring that you do it thoroughly. Not all writers do it. Some don't, and write about cardboard cut-outs instead of believable men and women. Some don't, and find themselves putting long lifeless chunks of description into their novel when a character or location first features, instead of dropping in telling details one by one.

(A warning: though it's good technique to intersperse

description with dialogue and action, you do need to give the reader enough information to enable him or her to visualize a character on, or very soon after, their first appearance – or not at all. If a reader has for 200 pages been thinking of Ivor as tall and brown-eyed, she doesn't want to be told on page 201 that he is actually short, fair and blue-eyed. Telling her on page 201 that Ivor flops down in his favourite armchair after a hard day's detecting and puts a Mozart sonata on the stereo is fine, however – so long as it leads her to think, 'Of course, that's precisely the music Ivor would choose,' or 'Good heavens, I hadn't realized that Ivor liked Mozart,' rather than 'I can't believe that a man like Ivor would ever pick *that* kind of music!')

Your résumé will of course include a physical description, so that you won't give your hero blue eyes at the start of the book and brown eyes at the end. It can usefully include much more as well. What kind of school did he attend? What did his parents do for a living, and where did they live? What are his hobbies? What make of car does he drive? Is he easygoing or short-tempered? A womanizer? Jewish, Christian, atheist? A smoker or non-smoker? What does he drink, and what is his favourite food? These, and dozens of other details, must gel together to create a rounded, believable character.

Many of these facts you may never refer to. The point is that when you do mention a detail, it must fit with, or extend in a believable way, your readers' conception of the character. Would Ivor prefer to listen to Dylan or Debussy, Springsteen or Stravinsky? Is he a good swimmer? Can he ride a bike (and is there one in his garden shed)? If you don't know him well enough to say, how are you going to make your readers feel that they know him, and care about what he does and how he feels?

The first words your heroine utters must be as fully in character as her parting shot, in both phrasing and meaning. Is Daphne the sort of girl who would fling the door open crying, 'Darling, do come in,' or the sort who would peer suspiciously through the keyhole before calling out, 'Who is it? I'm not going to release the security chain until I know.' You need to know before you make her speak, so that her character will come across clearly right from the start.

CHAPTER 7
The deal

It's a great thrill when a publisher offers to publish your first book, but this isn't the time to get carried away. Before you say an unequivocal 'yes please', it's important for you to know what kind of a deal you are being offered. Will the book appear in the form you expect it to (and in the bookshops you expect it to)? Will your payment be what you expect? Is this a fair and reasonable offer, or might you do better elsewhere?

I cannot go into detail here about every aspect of publishers' contracts. I can only explain the general economics of the process, and some of the points to watch out for.

Any contract should be vetted carefully. It is advisable for you to ensure that this is done before you sign, particularly if substantial sums of money are involved. If you use a literary agent, they will perform this task for you. Some literary agents will have written the contract themselves. The Society of Authors will provide detailed comments (often in letters several pages long) on contracts, free of charge, to authors who are members. (You can apply to join the Society as soon as you are offered your first contract.) Another option is to consult your solicitor, but this is expensive, and you may not find their advice helpful or easy to act upon if they are not already familiar with publishing contracts.

Ian McLachlan took an admirably cautious approach when he was offered a contract for his first book, *Final Flights*:

> I think I was careful before I signed anything, and read the contract through. I've got a friend who's a solicitor and I passed it over to him. I read through the Society of Authors' pamphlet on publishing contracts [available to non-members at a small charge]. And okay, while the deal

> wasn't from my point of view attractive, it was the same as everybody else seemed to be getting.

McLachlan's book is based on his hobby of aviation research. His research was expensive and time-consuming, and it was also expensive for him to produce his highly illustrated typescript. He is a realistic and organized author, who accepts that the book will probably not make him a profit.

Copyright

You automatically own the copyright in your own work. It is not necessary to register your copyright, except in the USA. The permission of the copyright holder is necessary before anybody else can produce copies of the work in any form, including not only books but serializations, television and film adaptations, translations and so on.

You can assign your copyright to another individual or company. If you do this, you lose all subsequent rights in your work in favour of the assignee. Individuals who work for an organization often assign copyright in written work carried out as part of their employment. Writers who are hired on a freelance basis to produce a specific piece of work are again often obliged to surrender their copyright as a condition of their hire.

Some books are produced on this basis. The writer is paid a fixed fee to produce a fixed amount of work, and that is the end of the deal. This method is often used for the highly illustrated, tightly laid-out books produced by 'package' publishers, who typically produce several editions of each book in a variety of languages, which they sell to end-publishers in different countries. The writer is then working on much the same basis as the photographer, illustrator, book designer, editor, and others involved in the book production process.

Packaged books may sell millions of copies, but the writer still only receives a fixed fee. Some writers find this an acceptable way of doing business, as long as the fee is adequate in the first place.

Cookery book writer Josephine Bacon has always worked

in this way – and she's happy with it. Her advice to would-be authors is, 'Don't get on your high horse about copyright and royalties.'

Other authors are less happy. Juri Gabriel's first book, *Victoriana* (published by Hamlyn) sold around 150,000 copies. He received a single flat fee for his work, that amounted to far less than a normal royalty on 150,000 copies. He felt in retrospect that he should have been able to share in its success, and that it was not reasonable that all the rewards should go to the publisher.

That the author should share in success is an accepted principle in virtually all other types of publishing. Reputable publishers (except for packagers) do not generally ask to buy your copyright. Instead, they contract for the right to produce and sell copies of your work (sometimes with limitations – for example, in specific formats, or for sale only in specific territories) in return for paying you a royalty on each copy sold.

Where you are offered a deal involving sale of copyright, my advice is to approach it with caution. Sometimes the sum offered is laughably small. Robert Hale, for example, regularly offer a flat £100 for romances. You may be grateful for their offer if your book has already received a string of rejections, but few authors would choose this type of deal if other possibilities were still open to them.

Janet Hutcheon sold her first book to Hale, under a pseudonym:

> I met a girl who'd just had her first book accepted, and I thought, oh, how wonderful, and Robert Hale had done it. I heard that they were good with first novels. I sent a synopsis and individual chapters to about three publishers, and Robert Hale were the first to reply saying they were interested. So I forgot about the other two and I just went on with them.
>
> They pay you peanuts, absolutely nothing. I wouldn't write another one for them. It was six months' work for £100 flat, which is ridiculous. They only print 800 copies and they only go to libraries. This is the sort of thing that you never read anywhere, inside information on publishers. I would have liked to have known that Robert Hale were only going to distribute it to libraries, and that it would never be sold in a bookshop anywhere.

Advances and royalties

Your royalty on direct sales of your book (that is, sales from your publisher to a wholesaler or bookseller or both) is normally expressed as a proportion of the selling price of the book. This is the only really satisfactory basis for calculating a royalty: complex accounting methods make formulas based on proportions of the publisher's profit or net receipts much less reliable.

Sometimes different formulas are used for indirect sales (for example, sales of unbound sheets to a library binder; book club sales; sales of bound or unbound copies to an overseas publisher). You may need expert advice to tell you whether the terms set out in your contract are fair.

Royalty percentages vary, depending upon the type of book and its expected sales: 10 per cent for hardbacks, and 7½ per cent for paperbacks, are typical figures. Often the percentage is increased to 15 or even 20 per cent if sales reach a certain level. In some circumstances the amount is lower. Mills & Boon contracts often specify 4 per cent on UK paperback sales, and 2 per cent on sales of any North American paperback edition. However, their sales are generally high, their authors' overall returns are comparatively good, and they have little direct competition, so they are in a strong bargaining position.

Royalties are paid after a book is published, and after its sales have been calculated. Books are often sent to booksellers on a sale or return basis, and in this case it is difficult or impossible to judge sales accurately. A proportion of the royalty may be held back to allow for returns.

Most publishers make up their accounts every six months (to the end of December and June), and their contracts typically allow them a further three months in which to pay the author. Sometimes the period is longer: Mills & Boon take five months.

If your book is accepted by a publisher in, say, January 1990, it may not be published until January 1991. The first royalty period will then end on 30th June 1991, and your royalties will probably not be paid until late in September 1991. That's a long time to wait for your payment. It's to your advantage if your contract specifies that you will be paid an advance on royalties.

Advances are normally paid at any or all of three points:

- when the contract is signed;
- when the completed typescript is delivered, and
- when the book is published.

The proportion paid at any of these times is normally open to negotiation. The advance is normally made against all monies due, to include payments on subsidiary rights as well as royalties. When your advance has been earned, you can expect (depending on the terms of your contract) to receive your proportion of subsidiary rights payments immediately they are received by the publisher, rather than waiting to the end of the next royalty period.

Advances are not returnable if your royalties do not reach the same figure, as frequently happens. (Nor are they normally returnable if you deliver a typescript that fits the contract specification, but the publisher fails to publish it.) So the advance represents a minimum sum that you are certain to earn from publication of the book, and it also represents part of the publisher's irretrievable investment in your book.

Publishers naturally make every effort to recoup their investment, so a large advance doesn't only swell your immediate bank balance, it also ensures that the publisher will make a substantial effort to publicize and sell your book. Though good publishers make some attempt to publicize and sell every book they publish, the scale of the effort inevitably varies.

If one author has received a £100,000 advance, and another a £1,000 advance, it's not hard to guess which one the publicity department will try to get onto television chat shows; which one will get the full-page colour ads in *The Bookseller*, the publicity tour and the display material; and which one will be expected to settle for a five-minute interview on the local radio station, and a short piece in the local free newspaper.

The size of your advance

There's no standard size for advances. Most publishers fix

them individually for each book, and it is up to the author or agent to try to negotiate them upwards. Since headline publicity goes to whopping advances, some would-be authors have a rather inflated idea of the sums involved. A few advances do reach well into six figures, but this is not the usual level for first novels, memoirs or non-fiction books of any kind. Every author should ask for an advance of some kind, but some authors still do not obtain advances, and if the expected sales are small it may be in three figures rather than four.

As a rule of thumb, publishers should (if pressed) agree to pay an advance of at least 50 per cent of the expected total royalties on the first printing. You can find out that figure by asking to look at the sales estimate, or asking how large the first print run will be, and the intended selling price.

Your cut

You may feel that the author's share of what a book earns is pitifully small. Many authors would heartily agree with you. It may help you to put the issue in perspective if you understand how the cover price of a book is distributed as income.

Publisher Tim Hely Hutchinson, writing in *The Author,* the Society of Authors' journal in Autumn 1988, estimated this to be a typical breakdown:

- *The trade discount* (i.e. the price at which the publisher sells to the wholesaler) averages 50 per cent, though it can vary considerably for different types of book.
- *Manufacturing costs* account for around 17 per cent, distribution and marketing for 8 per cent, and publishers' overheads for 10 per cent.
- *The author's royalty* share (assuming the advance is fully earned) averages 10 per cent, and that (if all goes according to plan) leaves 5 per cent for *the publisher's net profit*.

Rights

The rights that you sell to a publisher may be the full world rights (exclusive rights to publish the book anywhere, and in any form, or to sub-license other publishers to do so) or they may be far more restrictive.

There is no advantage for you in trying to restrict the rights that you grant, unless you are in a position to sell the remaining rights successfully. If you use a literary agent, s/he may well wish to reserve foreign or other major rights, in order to sell those separately. If you do not, and if you are a British author based in Britain, how do you propose to find an American publisher for your book? Unless you have a ready answer, it will probably be as well to let your British publisher attempt to find one for you. (Your contract should specify that you receive a high proportion of the American publisher's payments to your British publisher.)

Territories and foreign publishers

Books written in English are sold in what are effectively three different markets: the exclusive British market, the exclusive American market, and the open market.

Traditionally, the exclusive British market has consisted of the old British Commonwealth, with the addition of a few countries that have never been part of the Commonwealth, but where British influence has been strong. The exclusive American market has consisted of the US and its colonies and protectorates. Canada has been included in the American market for books originating in the US, and in the British market for books originating in the UK.

Today these old demarcations have faded, and the countries included in each market may be individually negotiated. In addition, the advent of the single European market in 1992 is likely to have a substantial impact, and may indeed totally destroy this system. Its precise effect is not clear at the time of writing. The situation can also be different for books that are initially published in Australia or New Zealand.

In the exclusive British market, the British publisher of the book has sole selling rights. In the exclusive American market, the American publisher has sole selling rights, and in the open market the two are free to compete.

Naturally you will hope for your English-language book to be published in both the US and Britain, unless it is evident that it has no potential for American sales. This means that you will need both a British and an American publisher. Sometimes the same multinational organization publishes books in both markets, but this is rarely automatic, even when you sell your book to a multinational firm such as Viking-Penguin. A less satisfactory alternative is for your British publisher to arrange a distribution deal with an American publisher. (In this case, copies of the book as printed for the British market are shipped out to, and sold in, the US.)

Publishers in other languages generally, but not invariably, acquire exclusive world rights (to produce and sell editions in that language) in the books they publish.

Hardback and paperback rights

It is common for all British rights in a book – including hardback rights, paperback rights, serial rights, book club rights, anthology rights, radio, television, film and video rights, and various less valuable rights like large-print and talking book rights – to be granted to your British publisher.

Again, there's no advantage in withholding any of these rights unless you have an agent who is willing to sell them separately, or you yourself have a clear idea what you will do with them – or have already disposed of them elsewhere. If there is a real possibility of substantial earnings from any of these rights (maybe a film producer has expressed some interest in the book), then you will naturally use this as a bargaining factor when negotiating your deal.

A few leading authors (including Jeffrey Archer and Frederick Forsyth) have made a decision not to permit book club editions of their works. The author's return on each copy sold by book clubs is notoriously tiny. It won't generally benefit a new author, however, to begin by following their example. You will more likely think yourself fortunate to receive the publicity and extra sales generated by a book club, even though you are unlikely to earn a substantial sum from these sales.

The traditional method for selling British rights is for the author or agent to offer both hardback and paperback rights to a hardback publisher. This publisher is then free either to publish both hardback and paperback editions, or to sub-license the rights to the paperback edition to a specialist paperback house.

Today the paperback sales of many books heavily out-number their hardback sales, and the advances paid for paperback rights are often considerably larger than the advances paid for hardback rights – especially in fiction. Increasingly, too, authors who can expect substantial paperback sales want to be able decide which imprint will publish their paperback, and not to leave this to their hardback publisher. In these circumstances, the old system makes less and less sense.

If a hardback publisher pays you, say, £1,000 for the full rights to your first novel, and then sub-licenses the paperback rights to another publisher for £100,000, the contract may specify that they pass on to you only 50–60 per cent of this payment. They will pocket £40,000–£50,000, and make a substantial profit before they've sold a single copy of the hardback. True you'll receive £50,000–£60,000, and doubtless won't be heartbroken, but you may justly feel that you might have arranged things differently and obtained a larger share.

In cases like this, where the sums involved are substantial, it can make sense for you or your agent to sell hardback and paperback rights separately, or to sell both to a house capable of publishing in hardback *and* paperback.

However, it's rare for an unknown and unagented first-time author to break into this league.

Other contract issues

Among the other points you will need to check in your contract are:

- *Licence period*. This is the period for which you grant rights to the publisher. Traditionally this has been for the full copyright period (that is, until fifty years after your death) but there is a move to reduce it to a fixed period of, typically, twenty years. This condition can be very important if you hope to embark on a long writing career which may involve changes of publisher. A relatively short licence period is to your advantage, but many publishers strongly resist this move.

- *Undertaking to publish.* Particularly if you are being commissioned from a synopsis, you must ensure that the publisher gives a firm undertaking to publish the book. You should not need to accept any clause making publication dependent upon their approval of the typescript.
- *Timescale.* Ensure that your deadline is one you can comfortably meet (and that you will be able to meet the timescale for checking proofs).

  The publisher should also indicate a timescale within which they publish your book. A year is a normal time from delivery to publication, unless the book is particularly complex to produce. If a longer period is specified, why? Can you negotiate it downwards? Will you be paid your full advance in, or before, a year after delivery?
- *Illustrations, quotations and index.* All of these, if required, can be costly and time-consuming to produce. Whose responsibility is it to produce them? Who is to pay for them? Do not commit yourself to these costs without negotiating: you may be able to persuade the publisher to bear part or all of them.
- *Consultation.* It can – and should – be written into the contract that neither the title nor the text will be altered without your consultation and agreement. You can also specify that you should be consulted about the jacket and blurb (though you will rarely be allowed a veto), and the publicity plans.
- *Author's copies.* Authors are generally sent a small number (usually six) of free copies of each edition. It's worth while to try to negotiate this number upwards, particularly if you will need to present several copies to people who have helped with your research. You can normally buy further copies at trade price, but on con-

dition that you do not sell them. (This clause is included at the insistence of booksellers.)

- *Remainders.* The publisher has the right to sell off stocks if sales fall, but you can – and should – ensure that this will not be done too quickly after publication (a year is a typical period), and that you will have an opportunity to buy surplus stocks before they are disposed of.
- *Options.* An option clause (that is, for the publisher to have first refusal of your next work) may seem flattering, but it is to the publisher's advantage, not to yours, as they make no commitment to publish. If possible, have this clause removed. If it remains, resist any attempt to specify that the next book(s) should be offered on the same terms: maybe you will be far more 'bankable' by the time your next novel is ready. The terms of your next contract should be 'to be mutually agreed'.
- *Termination.* A good termination clause is to your advantage: it will ensure that you can try to place your work elsewhere if the publisher lets it go out of print. You should not accept any clause which obliges you to repay any unearned advance, or otherwise pay the publisher, before recovering your rights on termination of the contract.

Negotiating contracts

Even the most immutable-looking printed contract can be amended. Some agents successfully insist that publishers accept the agent's contract form, rather than their own; all agents, and many unrepresented authors, negotiate over contract clauses. John Hedgecoe takes a forthright approach:

> I'm rather cynical about contracts. If you don't like a clause you just cross it out. One always crosses out about six and they want two of them back in.

The Minimum Terms Agreement

Over recent years, the Society of Authors and the Writers' Guild have been negotiating to try to persuade UK publishers to accept a model contract known as the Minimum Terms Agreement. This is a slightly misleading name, because several of the clauses in the MTA are considerably more favourable to the author than those in the average publisher's contract.

Many publishers have strongly resisted attempts to impose the MTA, with particular argument raging around the clause which specifies a negotiable length of licence. However a number of firms have signed the Agreement, including W. H. Allen, BBC Publications, Bloomsbury, Faber, Hamish Hamilton and Headline. If you contract with one of these firms, you can expect to receive a contract which conforms with the MTA stipulations. If you contract with a firm that has not accepted the MTA, you may still find it helpful to know which conditions writers' organizations are pressing to have accepted. These are among the specifications of the MTA:

- Either party has the opportunity to ask for the terms of the contract to be reviewed every ten years.
- Any income received from sub-licences is to be paid immediately, once the advance in earned.
- The cost of indexing, if not done by the author, is to be shared equally between author and publisher.
- The author is to receive 12 free copies of a hardback, and 20 of a paperback.
- The author is to be informed of the size of the print run.
- There is to be full discussion prior to signing the contract about illustrations, quotations, etc., and agreement as to who will pay. Normally the publishers will pay some or all of the costs involved.
- There is to be full consultation on all illustrations, the jacket, the blurb and the publication date.
- The author is to be invited to make suggestions for publicity, and to be shown the proposed distribution list for review copies.

- The author is to be consulted in full before any major sub-licences are granted.

The minimum royalty scale proposed in the MTA (not applicable for some specialist and heavily illustrated books) is:

- *For hardbacks*: 10 per cent to 2,500 copies; 12½ per cent to 5,000 copies and 15 per cent thereafter, on published price (home sales) or publisher's receipts (exports). On small reprints, this may revert to 10 per cent.
- *On home (mass market) paperbacks*: a minimum of 7½ per cent rising to 10 per cent after 50,000 copies. *On export paperbacks*: a minimum of 6 per cent of the published price. If the paperback rights are sub-licensed, the author to receive at least 60 per cent of income, rising to 70 per cent at a point to be agreed.
- *Minimum percentages to be paid to the author from sub-license income are*:

* American rights:	85 per cent
* Translations:	80 per cent
* First serial rights:	90 per cent
* TV and radio dramatizations:	90 per cent
* Film rights:	90 per cent
* Anthology and quotation rights:	60 per cent
* TV and radio readings:	75 per cent
* Merchandizing:	80 per cent

Non-contract issues

Even the best consultation clause in a contract cannot force a publisher to produce a type of book they do not wish or intend to produce. You are much more likely to be satisfied with your publisher's performance if you ensure, before you sign the contract, that you know precisely how they propose to produce, distribute and publicize your book. When you are offered a contract and advance, the publisher will almost certainly have already done some preliminary costings and sales estimates. You can – and should – ask to see them.

In what format will your book be published? What is the planned selling price? How large will the first print run be? Does the publisher plan to issue it in hardback, paperback or both? Will hardback and paperback come out simultaneously? When will they come out? Does the publisher plan to sub-contract any of the rights? All these, and many other issues, may affect your attitude to the contract, and your eventual satisfaction with the deal you receive.

Of course your publisher cannot guarantee your sales figures, but your sales figures will probably be closely related to the publisher's expectations. If your publisher doesn't expect your book to be a bestseller, chances are it won't be. Possibly another publisher would see a bigger potential for it, and would commit greater resources to realizing that potential.

Maybe you are not concerned about massive sales, but you will still want to know how your book will look – and you might well prefer a different publisher who proposes to issue it with a better binding, better quality paper and more illustrations.

If your book is still to be written, or if you hope to receive editorial help with subsequent books, then it will be important to you to meet the editor who is assigned to you, and to ensure that you are in sympathy with them. The editor may indicate to you that some changes will be required to your synopsis or typescript. You should be clear about the nature and extent of those changes before you sign a contract. Sometimes publishers demand very considerable changes, an issue I discuss in more detail in Chapter 12.

There are other considerations, too, about which you cannot ask your publisher directly. Is the firm financially stable? Is it efficient? Are its production standards good? Does it pay over monies due promptly? Your contract may be exemplary, but will the firm keep to it?

You can often find at least partial answers to these questions by talking to other authors, or by reading the trade press. In the UK *The Author* (free to members of the Society of Authors, on sale to non-members) is an invaluable source of information. *The Bookseller* (expensive, but available in most libraries) contains a great deal of trade gossip.

The Society of Authors occasionally polls its members to obtain just this kind of information. The results of its latest poll were published in Autumn 1988. Authors were invited to grade their publishers from '1' (bad) to '5' (excellent) in each of sixteen categories.

The overall grades were highest for 'strict adherence to terms of contract' and lowest for 'consultation/information about going out of print and remaindering', an issue that may seem distant now, but that can be of vital importance in the long run. 'Quality and efficiency of promotion/publicity' also scored poorly. Overall, the verdict of Michael Legat, who analysed the survey returns, was that 'the biggest problem in author/publisher relations is a failure to communicate.'

The Society of Authors acts for members who experience severe difficulty with their publisher – often in receiving royalties and subsidiary rights payments when due – and occasionally advises members to avoid dealings with firms which have a very poor record on such issues.

Paying to be published

You may have seen classified or small display advertisements in literary magazines and heavyweight newspapers, inviting hopeful authors to submit their work to publishers on the look-out for new talent. Sometimes these specify a particular interest in poetry, short stories and autobiographies.

That should act as a warning sign, since these are all notoriously hard-to-place forms of writing.

Reputable publishers do not advertise for authors in this way. The receive plenty of submissions without advertising. The only publishers who place this form of advertisement are 'vanity' or 'subsidy' publishers.

These firms invariably assure those who send them material that it is of publishable standard, and they offer to publish it. But, they continue, there's a commercial risk involved that they cannot bear alone. Would the author care to invest in the enterprise? In other words, you are being asked to pay to be published.

Those who pay do indeed get published, but rarely in the way they hoped. Vanity presses sometimes contract to print sizeable number of copies – but often the small print reveals that only a small proportion of these will be bound. Their books are not reviewed in reputable newspapers and magazines. Their distribution system is often poor or non-existent, and in any case few bookshops agree to stock books like these. Your book won't become a bestseller; it won't even become a moderate seller. It may sell no copies at all, except for those you take yourself.

If you've suffered rejection after rejection, and hunger to see your work in print, this kind of offer may be tempting. Maybe you have good reasons for considering it carefully. Your work may be impeccably researched, but too specialized to be a commercial proposition; you may have written memoirs or a family history that will interest only your own family, but interest them intensely; it may be poetry that does not please today's poetry editors, but has great sentimental importance for you and yours.

It's understandable that in circumstances like these, you may be prepared to pay to be published. Even so, there's no reason for you pay over the odds. You don't need a pretend publisher with no distribution system. You would be far better going to a local printer and telling him what you want.

A vanity publisher will do no more for you than a good editor, designer and printer would do. They'll most likely do less, charge you far more, and take a hefty whack of the profit from any sales you make yourself.

If you have reason to finance the publication of your book, then I strongly advise you to avoid the vanity presses, and publish it yourself. This is entirely possible, and can be very satisfying. I discuss the experiences of some authors who have tried it in chapter 14.

CHAPTER 8
Writing methods

There's no rule about how you should go about writing your book. Successful authors vary widely in their methods, and there's no particular practice that seems to work best. One thing, however, they almost all have in common. They keep at it. Jasper Ridley:

> I always say, which is quite true, that I write whenever I'm not doing anything else. By that I mean, whenever I haven't got a meeting, a lecture, a dinner party or something. Unfortunately I once said this in an interview with a newspaper editor, who wrote, 'Jasper Ridley takes his writing very leisurely. He only writes when he has nothing else to do.'
>
> In fact I work – when I'm hectically finishing a book I sometimes work 12, 13, 14 hours a day. I suppose I normally work about nine hours a day.

It wouldn't be possible to research and complete a very long historical biography without a regular work schedule. A short novel probably won't take nearly as long to write, but with fiction it's particularly important to keep writing every day, so that the story and characters remain uppermost in your mind, and you reduce the risk of being 'blocked'.

Frederick Forsyth is a super-disciplined writer. When he's writing a book he aims to get up at around 6.30 am. He'll 'moon around' for a while, drink some coffee, read over the previous day's work, and be at his desk by 8 am. He then writes – onto a portable typewriter – until around 1 pm. He does little revision, and reckons to complete half a chapter in each session: so one of his 20 chapter books is actually written in around 40 working days.

Romance writer Elizabeth Oldfield works more slowly: each of her 50,000 word romances takes her three months on average. She works from 9 am to 6 pm each day, and aims to complete about a chapter a week (of an eight- or nine-chapter book), though she doesn't set herself a target each day. Sometimes the work flows smoothly, she finds, while 'sometimes you get bogged down'. But she rarely if ever abandons a book halfway through: she will always resolve her difficulties somehow.

Not all authors are such early risers. Jeremy Leland:

> I write mostly at night in the still, small hours. I don't function well in the early morning. The main requirement is a good supply of fuel: cigarettes, cigars, cups of coffee, flagons of beer. I work directly onto a word processor, and sit perched on a Balans stool, theoretically to ease the back, though I'm not convinced. I imagine this must be a pretty average profile of a writer today, plus the obligatory reclining cat.

By day, Leland regularly does voluntary work for organizations such as the Citizen's Advice Bureau. Only a few authors write as a full-time occupation: the majority, and virtually all beginners, have to fit their writing around their day job. Even so, it's useful to fall into some kind of routine, however loose.

Pauline Kirk works full-time – and has teenage children – and wouldn't want to give up work however successful she became as a novelist, because 'it would cut me off from the stimulus of other people'. It took her two years to write her first novel to be published (the second she wrote), *Waters of Time*, a historical saga. She's used to writing wherever and whenever she can – in bed, in the bath, in the car – and though she has just bought a word processor, she expects to keep on drafting by hand because she cannot possibly use the word processor in all those places.

Writer and journalist Patsy Westcott (her latest book is *Finding Someone to Love*) tries to do her writing in the mornings – 'I'm more creative then' – leaving her afternoons free for telephone calls: it's cheaper. If she manages to get back to work in the evenings, she will generally edit what she has written that morning.

Some writers find that collaborations help to discipline them to work. Sheila Dainow, a specialist in interpersonal communication skills, has written three books – two with Jill Cox, and one with Caroline Bailey (*Developing Skills with People*). She enjoys working with somebody rather than alone, and has found both collaborations 'amazingly problem-free'.

Sheila's method is to get together with her co-author and talk through a synopsis. They then 'develop a kind of rhythm', agreeing who will draft which section of the book. Each writer sends her drafted sections to the other for comment and amendment, then they meet up to discuss the work again, before one of them prepares a final version.

Caroline Buchanan wrote *The Sensuous Slimmer* with her long-term friend Sandra Sedgbeer. They are very different people, she claims, but again the collaboration worked well. Like Dainow and Cox, they worked by drafting alternate chapters and then swapping them for editing.

Disciplining and motivating strategies

The best strategies for keeping yourself going are the simplest. Try to set aside a regular time for writing. Try to write frequently – every day if possible – even if it's only for a few minutes. Write regularly – letters, diaries, anything – so that you are in the habit of letting your thoughts flow onto paper.

Many writers start their day's work by reading over what they have written the day before. This is a good strategy, but don't overdo it. If you start back at page 1 every day, you'll spend all your time revising and none carrying your story forwards. The previous day's work should be sufficient to remind you where you left off, and to get you in the mood to continue.

Some writers find that daily word targets help them, while many more find their thoughts concentrated by the approach of a deadline. Deadlines must be taken seriously. Whatever the myths, it is not acceptable to miss them regularly. Non-fiction author Ian McLachlan:

> I found that the timescale element was actually good. Somebody said right, first of June, that is the deadline, and it's amazing how that focuses the mind. Whereas if it had

been left to me I'd have been writing it for ever.

Biographer Michael Holroyd is not so keen:

> There is an argument that deadlines concentrate the mind wonderfully, that one can do much more than one thinks, and having got a habit of work one relaxes too much into it, is rather indulgent to oneself. I think I have a general anxiety which keeps me from relaxing too much. But on the whole deadlines don't work terribly well for me. I wish they did.
>
> I have a deadline now for Shaw, which is about 18 months on, and I notice I'm always calculating whether I'm ahead or not, and I'm not sure that's all that good. I like letting things have their natural pace – and I'm very keen to finish. I want to complete the thing, I know I can, there's nothing holding me back. Deadlines are publishers' friends, a lifeline is what I need.

Writers without a commission don't have a deadline imposed by a publisher. Some find it helpful to assign their own deadline, either picking a significant date ('I'll have this wretched novel out of the way by Christmas') or by entering their work for a literary competition.

Literary competitions are good motivating factors in themselves, especially for the winners. Often, success in a competition can provide a first step to publication.

Cynthia Harrod-Eagles, novelist:

> A fellow student at London University came and told me there was a notice on the noticeboard about NEL's Young Writers' Competition, for a previously unpublished writer. I rushed off home and finished my novel *The Waiting Game*. You had to send two copies, so the man in the next-door bedsitter photocopied it for me, and I got it in absolutely on the deadline.
>
> I won joint first prize – they asked us to share it, I think they were realizing they'd been rather too generous with the prize money – and that was my first published book.

Short-story competitions help some writers to realize that it's possible to get into print. Jean Rennie, author of *Every Other Sunday*, a memoir about her years in service:

> I was in hospital, and my mother got me a *People's Friend*

> magazine, which had a competition for a summer love story. I asked her to bring me an exercise book, and I wrote this wee love story. I'd never done anything like it before. I had a letter from them saying that I hadn't won the competition, but they were keeping the story for publication at ordinary rates. I was thrilled to be published for the first time.

Fifty years later, Rennie is still an inveterate competition-enterer.

Poetry competitions, too, can give newcomers a leg up the ladder. Colin Rowbotham received around a hundred rejection slips when he started submitting poems to magazines, then he won first prize in a small competition and had his winning entry published. Subsequently he found success in a couple more competitions, met the judges, and things began to fall into place for him. His first collection of poems, *Total Recall*, was published by the small Littlewood Press in 1987.

Encouragement by family, friends or other writers is vital to everyone. A suggestion from a friend or relation gets many writers started. Jasper Ridley:

> I'd just got married and my wife had heard of Nicholas Ridley, the Protestant Martyr. Actually it is rather doubtful whether he is connected with our family, but we'd always thought he was. She said, is there a good biography of him? I said, there isn't one, so she said, why don't you write one? So I did.

Ridley's biography of his namesake became his first published book. Jeremy Leland unashamedly looks for lots of praise:

> Encouragement is what counts. First book came out during a disintegrating marriage, but on reappraisal it looks as though subsequent partners may have been chosen for assiduity with the admiration.

Kathy Page, another novelist, relies on a small writing group for more abrasive feedback:

> I went along to an evening class. Sometimes you were set things to do, but mostly you were supposed to do things and then discuss them. I really got stuck into it more or less

> straightaway, and I wanted to write a novel after about three weeks.
>
> We left the evening class in the end and made up a writing group. We all used to write. Every three weeks I'd read another chunk of novel, get a lot of criticism and do it again. That's how my first novel got written, very much with continuous feedback all the way through.

Other writers find drawbacks to this type of consultation process. 'I couldn't imagine discussing a book in detail with anyone except my editor,' says Pat Barr. Michael Holroyd agrees:

> What you suddenly think of, after a decade or so, is, have I run off the track? Am I on course at all? I feel a lonely figure jogging along. Is anyone interested at all?
>
> So when I did show the first version [of my biography of Shaw] to my agent, I felt a tremendous relief. Apart from flattery or encouragement, there seemed a really positive response, I hadn't been making a complete fool of myself. There's always that risk that you run when you work alone.
>
> If you can get away with not showing it to people, on the whole I think that's better. There are exceptions, for example if somebody has specialist knowledge of something, but I think it's bad to talk away one's book, or as it were, publish it amongst one's friends prematurely, or amongst other writers prematurely. In a way that takes away from the impulse to write it. These things have to be done in solitude.

Pen and ink or word processor?

Again, writers vary enormously. Their preferences depend partly on background – journalists know how to type, at least after a fashion, but many other writers don't – and largely on their tendency to revise. Michael Holroyd again:

> I write in ink – ink and ballpoint pen, whatever. I don't actually grind my own ink, but it's pretty primitive stuff. Not altogether legible, and it goes through several drafts. Lots of crossings-out. Then it goes to the typing stage, and

either I type it out, or more recently I have got a typist, who needed the work, to do that and then return it to me.

I try and look at it as if it were somebody else's work. That's the useful thing about an anonymous typescript as opposed to one's personal handwriting. The final typescript with its corrections then goes to a word processor expert who puts it on disc from which it is published.

This feeling that a typed or word-processed draft becomes anonymous is common to many writers. Pat Barr, historian, biographer and novelist:

I have a word processor now, but the first draft I still write with pen and paper. I think there's something about the business of actually putting it down on paper manually that makes it work better. It does for me, anyway. Part of the whole process of writing is actually to write.

I always feel that it's too kind of finished if it goes onto a typewriter. I do quite a lot of crossing out, and I have my own system of inserts with coloured pencils.

The first draft is The Draft absolutely. Of course one changes and revises a bit, but I always feel when the first one's done it's done, more or less.

My last book – that was non-fiction, and the first time I'd had a word processor – I was able to get from that first draft to more or less finished on the word processor. So that took out an interim draft which I always used to do before I did the final, or maybe two interim drafts. But nevertheless the first draft is the absolute crucial thing.

This emphasis on the first draft is true for many writers, and it's important to use a medium that doesn't get in the way. Many writers who are comfortable with word processors like to compose straight onto the screen, but those who are not very familiar with a word processing system can find that getting the commands right is too much of a distraction from the real business of getting the words right.

For other writers, the first draft is more of a long synopsis. Novelist George Target:

I get a first draft down just anyhow, scribble it down, and then I have his marvellous couple of months playing with it, fiddling with it. I do what I call a paste-up. The biggest

> instruments I have are a pair of scissors and a paste pot. I cut it all up, page by page, and rearrange it. I try to do kaleidoscopic things, I like it to be multi-dimensional. I think if you give me 10,000 words I can turn it into 100,000 words in a very happy couple of months. But the first 10,000 are very difficult.

Even if the words in the first draft are roughly right, many writers do a great deal of revision before they get them absolutely right. Here the word processor can be a godsend, so long as you manage to see typed text as revisable. Colin Rowbotham uses a word processor for revising his poems:

> I started off writing longhand, on loose sheets so that I could revise easily. I'd put my best efforts into a binder. Then I taught myself to touch-type. I'd type my poem, then every time I changed a word I would retype it, so that I could see it without distraction, and feel the rhythm. Sometimes I would do this thirty or forty times. Now I edit my poems on my Amstrad word processor, and can print out a revised version much more quickly.

Not every writer has the patience to type forty drafts, especially of a long book. Using a word processor can encourage writers to do more revision. Cynthia Harrod-Eagles:

> I used to have to send my publishers four copies of my books, and I produced them by doing carbon copies. I couldn't bear to type anything more than once, and to correct anything through three carbons is terribly tedious, so I developed this method of thinking it all out very carefully first and then typing one final draft.
>
> I've worked with a typewriter since I was eleven, and consequently I never feel at ease writing longhand. I can't keep up with myself, it's too slow.
>
> I've only just gone over to a word processor. I was reluctant to change my work when I had a very heavy workload on in case it interfered with the flow, which in fact it did to an extent. The changeover took several months. But now I've got it I'm very happy with it.
>
> I don't revise in the sense of rewriting large sections, but I'm much more accurate about the exact words I use. When I had a typewriter I tended to leave things which I would perhaps have said another way, because I couldn't

> be bothered to make all the corrections. But now I read back every sentence, and if I think of a slightly better way of phrasing it, then of course I will correct it before I print it out. So I'm writing much more as I want to write.

Though Barbara Cartland is famed for dictating her books, few authors copy her. It's not easy to develop a good style while dictating, but some authors find this a useful process if it is combined with heavy revision. John Hedgecoe, photography writer:

> With some of my books I dictate the text to a working editor. They get it transcribed and do a first edit, and then it comes back to me. I do a lot of work on it to make sure it's what I wanted to say, and roughly to the right word count. With my sort of books you sometimes have to do an exact word count, so the text will fit in a tight layout.

Though all these working methods work well for their users, I'd recommend any beginning writer to acquire, and learn to use (and use effortlessly, before starting on your book) a word processor. It really does ease your work, and greatly simplifies the task of turning out several well-produced copies of your manuscript. Though some writers swear they'll never use one, almost all of those who have tried one have become enthusiastic converts.

Which word processor?

It's partly a matter of personal choice, partly one of finances. Word processors do vary considerably in style and capability, though, and I'd strongly advise you to consult other writers, read the specialist press, and to check out several before committing yourself.

The program is the important thing: programs vary much more than the computers on which they run. In choosing a computer, concentrate on the screen quality, the keyboard quality, and the disc capacity, as well as assessing the overall quality of construction and the servicing on offer. (Computers shouldn't break down all that often, and I don't recommend that you pay a fortune for a servicing contract.) A hard disc costs considerably more than floppy discs, but it is worth it for security and ease of use.

On the whole you get what you pay for, and some of the very cheap programs are extremely difficult to use. The extra few hundred pounds you pay for a top quality program will rapidly justify itself if you use it every day.

Ensure that you choose a program which will cope easily with long runs of text. Some are designed primarily for short business letters. If you're planning to revise heavily, you may find it helpful to have a program that will let you work with several drafts of a document – or several different documents – simultaneously.

Another basic requirement is a program with good file handling capabilities: ordering your files, backing up all files automatically, and ideally letting you search for text through a series of files.

A spelling checker is essential, even for good spellers, and a thesaurus is to be recommended. (Several top-of-the-range programs include them.) Outline processors are extremely useful tools for those working with highly structured text.

I've reviewed word processing programs regularly for over five years. I use *WordPerfect* myself, and that's the one I recommend to other writers. *Microsoft Word* is also highly recommended. I do not recommend *Locoscript*, the program that runs on some Amstrad computers: it's much more difficult to use.

Judging length

It's important to get the length of your book right, especially if you have been commissioned to write to a specific length. Beginners often find this difficult.

Most books contain between 50,000 and 200,000 words. A typical 200 page literary novel will contain 70,000–85,000 words, and a 400–500 page book maybe 150,000–200,000 words. That's the normal top limit, exceeded only by major academic works and blockbuster sagas. For anything else, it is over the top. Your first novel or autobiography is more likely to sell if you keep it under 100,000 words.

So how many typescript pages make up 100,000 words? It depends on your typesize and layout, but 200–250 words to a double-spaced page is typical. So a 100,000 word typescript will fill 400–500 pages.

If you write a great deal of short sentence dialogue, or use a lot of subheadings, your pages may contain fewer words. But publishers use a rule of thumb, they don't count every word, and your 400 page typescript will still add up to around 250 printed pages. Bear this in mind if you use a word count routine on a word processor. If you write choppy text, what you and your word processor take to be 50,000 words your publisher may take to be 55,000.

Try to aim at making your first draft slightly too long. It's easier to cut a manuscript than to extend it. Cutting improves most people's work: often a brief sentence is more elegant and lively than a longer one that says the same.

Jasper Ridley specifically thinks of his revision as a cutting process:

> I write a chapter at a time and I then cut it and shorten it probably by nearly 20 per cent, and make alterations. I then type it out. I suppose a chapter is about 6–7,000 words, so I would write that probably in two days. I'd then spend two days shortening and correcting, and two days typing. The shortening and correcting is the hardest part of it. I learned to type as a child, and a good job too, because by the time I've made these cuts and corrections no typist could read it.

Ian McLachlan had the opposite problem with his first book, *Final Flights*:

> One of the hardest things I think, particularly when you're writing as a beginner, is judging how big is 90,000 words? I didn't really know. So I wrote and then thought, I've got the book finished, and then I added up the number of words and found that I was nearly 20,000 words short. So that's where the final chapter appeared, called Wreckovery and Wreckology. I thought, well, there's plenty of material there, I'll just put in a chapter along those lines.

This extra chapter wasn't in the synopsis McLachlan had agreed with his publishers, but they happily accepted the complete typescript.

Handling research data

It's particularly difficult to write a very fact-filled narrative. If you keep stopping to look up a vital piece of information, you soon lose the flow of the writing.

It helps, of course, to plan your section or chapter carefully before you begin. Frederick Forsyth, who works to a detailed synopsis, sorts his research notes into chapter bundles. Technical details, street maps, road maps, are all clipped together. Anything that borders on the indecipherable he types out. Then when he comes to the scene where the bomb goes off, he can quickly and easily lay his hands on data about bombs, and feed it in without breaking his concentration.

Jasper Ridley takes this process a step further:

> After I've finished all the research I read the notes through to get them in my head. Then when I start writing I again read the notes through at the beginning of each particular chapter. But I then put the whole thing away and write a whole chapter without looking at the notes. When I'm actually writing, I've got all the ideas in my head and I want to put them down on paper, I cannot look up and see whether it was three weeks or four weeks. So I put a "3" in square brackets, and afterwards I look up to see if it was three or four weeks. Occasionally this involves rewriting a sentence.

George Target learned this process the hard way, when he was commissioned to write a biography of Bernadette Devlin:

> I'd never written a biography before and I was intimidated. I spent eleven months collecting material. I had about a hundredweight and a half of press cuttings and clippings and notes and histories of Ireland, you name it.
>
> I was miles behind schedule, I was completely overwhelmed by material, I was desperate. My wife said to me, throw it all away and start again. I didn't believe her, but I pushed it all to one side and took a pen and started writing. And it was all there. All that I needed to know was already in my mind.
>
> Afterwards we went through the material checking the quotations.

Revision

It's sometimes said that revision is the hallmark of the professional writer. Very few people manage to get the overall structure of a book, the structure of individual scenes or sections, the structure of sentences and the choice of words all right at the first attempt. Virtually all work can be improved through thoughtful revision, and I'd strongly advise you to learn good revision techniques. I discuss revision in greater depth in chapter 14.

That said, I reckon the real hallmark of a professional writer is careful preparation: and if you prepare what you're going to write meticulously, you won't waste nearly as much time on half-baked drafts as an unprepared writer will. A publisher won't be impressed if you tell them you've rewritten your masterpiece 50 times: they just want to receive a final version that's as good as you can make it.

CHAPTER 9
Big money

Only a minority of would-be authors write in the hope of turning out a world-wide bestseller. But some do; and some (far fewer) succeed.

Can you write a bestseller to order? The experts' quick answer is usually no. Patrick Janson-Smith of Transworld:

> This is a generalization, but the cynical approach to writing doesn't usually work. You know, can I write you a bestseller? I don't think I could say to any author who said, 'What shall I write?', write a bestseller. I mean, what is a bestseller?

What indeed? Really, there are several types of bestseller. There's the non-fiction 'big book': a massive authoritative tome on a subject with lots of popular appeal (e.g. Longman's *Chronicle of the 20th Century*), or perhaps a biography of a well-known figure, authorized (e.g. Michael Holroyd's biography of George Bernard Shaw) or scandalously unauthorized (e.g. Albert Goldman's *The Lives of John Lennon*). There's the 'airport novel': a thriller or saga with lots of excitement, lost of action, lots of sex. There are the latest works by established big-selling novelists like Frederick Forsyth, Jeffrey Archer and Catherine Cookson. There are 'silly books', often by (or at least, promoted by) television comics, which sell well as 'Christmas stocking fillers'. And there are unexpected big sellers like Stephen Hawking's *A Brief History of Time*, Rosemary Conley's *Complete Hip and Thigh Diet*, Aeron Clement's *The Cold Moons*.

It's also possible to make big money by writing huge quantities of moderate sellers: most notably, of Mills & Boon romances, which I discuss later in the chapter.

It's difficult to give guidance on the unexpected big sellers. If you have a hunch, then follow it: that's all you can say. It's equally difficult for a novice to break into the big league with a high-quality literary novel: it takes time to establish yourself in this field. 'Big books' tend to be commissioned from established big names. What's left? What many would-be bestselling authors try to write, the highly commercial 'airport' novel.

Airport novels

Sometimes so-called because they tend to appeal to people who are not heavy regular readers, but buy books to fill in dead time – on long journeys, or to read on the beach or holiday.

If there is a 'formula' bestseller, these books tend to be it. Vogues vary but the most recent distinguishable one has been for 'shopping and f***ing' novels. These are generally long, full of action, set in glamorous locations and populated with the rich, famous and beautiful, liberally sprinkled with sexual encounters (often highly bizarre), and even more liberally sprinkled with fashionable brand names. The plots are often preposterous, but there does have to *be* a plot.

Examples? Anything by Judith Krantz, Barbara Taylor Bradford, Jackie Collins, Shirley Conran. Sally Beauman's *Destiny* was a first novel (discounting a string of Mills & Boons) that made it big on this type of formula. Tom Wolfe's *The Bonfire of the Vanities* (also a first novel, though by a well-established journalist and non-fiction writer) was a variant on the same theme.

These novels are proof par excellence that the right (lowest common denominator of popularity) subject matter helps to sell novels. However, writing an airport novel demands far more than the ability to mention a few brand names and throw in the odd four-letter word. Sally Beauman, Shirley Conran and the rest are all highly professional writers, and their books are all, in their way, good books. Hundreds of thousands of readers – most of whom read through to the end, many of whom pass the paperback on to their friends and eagerly await the author's next offering – can testify to that. So can the dozens of editors who have to read through other writers' unsuccessful attempts to copy the formula.

What makes these novels good? It's not the authors' elegantly turned phrases or their original, poetic imagery. Readers of this type of novel don't look for fancy wording: sometimes they tolerate it, but generally they prefer the words to be a transparent medium that merely carries the story. Good writing in this context is writing that conveys meaning rapidly and effortlessly. This demands simple sentence constructions, short paragraphs, and a vocabulary that sends no one scurrying for the dictionary.

It's not the authors' deep psychological insights or subtle characterization. The characters are often crudely motivated. The plot can be ludicrous, so long as it has a consistency of its own. It is carried along via dramatic incidents – car crashes, shipwrecks, murders, adulteries – and fuelled by a basic, sometimes barely believable, but always powerful conflict situation, like Shirley Conran's 'Which one of you bitches is my mother?' or Jeffrey Archer's 'Which of these politicians is going to end up a Prime Minister?'

This fundamental conflict is backed up by endless sequences of smaller conflicts. We keep on turning the pages to find out who's going to go to bed with whom, who's going to find out what, who's going to get away with what. Good writing in this context means page-turning ability: readers keep on reading for just another few pages because they know that any time now they're going to find out whether she really does . . . it doesn't matter what she really does, so long as the question is there, and the reader is dying for the answer.

In order for the reader to want to find out, there's another basic requirement. The reader has to care about the characters. Highbrow critics may complain of cardboard characterization, but all these successful writers create characters who may be psychologically trite, but are always *believable*. They know how to slant their writing so that their readers are induced to care about their characters. They understand how important it is to draw characters in bold lines, and to keep them consistent.

Critics of Archer's *Kane and Abel* might complain that no real-life businessmen are remotely like Kane or Abel, but all the same, millions of readers come to feel they know Kane and Abel, would recognize them if they saw them in the street, can judge what they would say and not say, wear and not wear – and remember them years after they've finished reading about them.

Conveying character like this takes skill; it takes hard work; but above all, it demands sincerity. The writer has to believe in the character, has to see and hear and understand the character. Archer's Kane and Abel, Taylor Bradford's Emma Harte and all the rest couldn't come alive to readers as they do unless they had first come alive in the author's mind.

Action of this kind can't come alive unless the writer experiences it intensely, and has the skill to convey that intensity. Locations, glamorous or seedy, won't be clearly pictured in the reader's mind unless they have first been visualized in every detail by the writer.

This is what editors mean when they say they want sincerity. Authors who plan and write this kind of novel from the outside don't get it right. Sure, these fantastical plots need planning – but once the plot has been planned, the locations chosen, the characters named, you have to live with them in order to breathe life and vitality into them. Hold back your emotions and mutter cynically about trash, and you'll write a novel that is dull and condescending, not one that has the gripping quality that readers look for.

The same is true, of course, of novels with more realistic plots and more complex characters. Catherine Cookson doesn't put a sex scene on page one, but she holds her vast readership because she knows how to put across her character, convey settings, tell interesting stories and keep them moving, and keep her readers wanting to know what happens next. These are the qualities that really make a bestseller.

Against the formula?

Novelist Pat Barr hit the big time with *Jade*, her first novel:

> It really was a very big surprise. I thought I'd do well just to get a fiction book published – but it actually sold in the States, went into paperback, just did amazingly.

This was in spite of the fact that Barr refused a request to add more sex, because 'its done just for the sales really'.

Kenjiro, her second novel, also did well – though not quite as well. But by now, Barr had begun to see some of the disadvantages of being a big seller:

> *Kenjiro* sold for a big advance in the States, to Warner Bros. I was slightly overwhelmed by the amount, and in the contract they didn't make the stipulation that it should come out first in hardback. Warner Bros brought it out in a paperback cover that was just appalling. It made it look like soft porn. If I wrote soft porn I wouldn't mind, but this was just not that kind of book at all. It's not great literature but it's not a sort of romantic trashy book either.
>
> My latest novel, *Coromandel*, is set in South India in the 1830s. I've moved from a big canvas. The other two novels covered about ten to fifteen years each and a lot of characters, and for this one I wanted to have a go at a smaller scale, timescale and place scale and everything. So it takes place in three years, and it is fairly tight and small from that point of view.
>
> As a result, and because the subject doesn't much interest the Americans, it hasn't sold there at all, and I don't think it will. I knew this when I started it, and took the risk because it was something I wanted to do. It was also turned down by Corgi paperback, and my editor explained that they didn't like it because it didn't have a proper hero. My sort-of hero is gay.

Barr didn't begin by deliberately writing to a formula but almost by accident she hit on many of the formula elements that help to make a bestseller: the 'big' story, the appealing setting, the strong hero. The quality of writing and storytelling is just as good (if not better) in *Coromandel*: but it doesn't have these formula elements, and it doesn't have the same mass-market appeal simply because of that.

The romantic formula

Writing romantic fiction isn't an automatic passport to an AmEx Gold Card, but it can be, particularly for authors who write regularly for Mills & Boon. Some Mills & Boon authors come close to producing a new book a month, every month, year after year. Each book sells well, but not in blockbuster quantities: it's the accumulation of titles that builds up an author's reputation, and brings in the loot.

So a major requirement for a romance author is stamina. With this type of formula fiction, you cannot hope to produce a household-name bestseller on your first – or even your forty-first – attempt.

Romances that work have many of the features of airport novels that work. The plot must be strong, and believable, though not necessarily realistic. The characters should be consistent and reasonably sympathetic. There's no 'will she marry him?' suspense, since the happy ending is a basic requirement – and Mills & Boon like their heroes to be clearly identifiable from their very first appearance – but it's necessary to keep the reader wanting to know what happens next, and to move the story along fast, with plenty of incident.

Many romance readers devour the books in odd snatched moments, while the baby is napping or after doing the washing-up. (Any many read remarkable quantities of them: a dozen a month is common.) It's essential when writing this type of book to tell your story simply, so readers can follow it through numerous pickings-up and puttings-down. No fancy flashbacks, no huge cast of characters: they only confuse things.

Beyond all this, though, there's an iconic quality that makes a good romance. It's the stuff of fairytales, and like fairytales, the successful ones follow a tight formula.

American researcher Janice A. Radway has analysed the plots of a variety of romances that were rated especially highly by a sample of readers. Every one of them followed a 13-point, overall plot structure. (*Jane Eyre* fits it too.) First, the heroine finds herself in a situation in which she is afraid, isolated or insecure for some reason: perhaps her parents have just been killed,or she has started a new job, or travelled to an unfamiliar place. Then an antagonistic male appears, and the fireworks start . . . and so on until point 13 at the end of the book, where the heroine and the hero confess their love.

Obviously not every successful romance writer has read Radway's book (see Bibliography) or taken advantage of her

13-point plan. But somewhere, subconsciously, it has sunk in (not least because successful romance writers read, as well as write, lots and lots of romances) – and it is followed again and again, for the simple reason that it works. Readers get from it the romantic 'fix' that they want: and they keep on coming back for more of the same.

Best-selling non-fiction

Above all, the *subject* sells non-fiction. The biographies that shoot up the bestseller lists are biographies of famous people, not of nonentities. *The Complete Hip and Thigh Diet* sold because millions of women want to have slimmer hips and thighs. Photography, cookery and gardening books sell in their millions because millions of people take photographs, enjoy cooking interesting meals, and tend their gardens. Even with these broad topics, generality sells better than specificity. Best-selling photography writer John Hedgecoe is in an ideal position to provide it:

> A wide approach is the type of book that sells most of all. I've done everything from wedding photography to industrial photography to fashion photography. I did it for years. I did a heck of a lot of advertising, with almost every conceivable product from milk to whisky to cars to British travel. I've always loved photography over a wide canvas, from people to landscapes, still life. That's fairly rare, to be so broadly based.

Hedgecoe also attributes his success in an overcrowded field to his championing of a radically different approach to art and photography books:

> The first book I did was on the sculptor Henry Moore. The normal art book then was one page with two half-page pictures on it, and a page of text at the side. I wanted to do it much more as a pictorial biography of Henry Moore. It was twelve years before it was published – not that nobody would do it, but they wouldn't do it the way that I wanted to do it. It was a time when books cost £1.50, hardbacks, or £2, and when it did come out it cost £12.
>
> We changed art books with that, and we also did it with

> the photography books. Before mine came out they were very dry, with maybe half a dozen pictures. The one that we did, the first one, is still the book that everybody has copied, with extended captions and pictures.

Topical books sell, but it's authoritative books that keep on selling year after year. There are no short-cuts to writing authoritative non-fiction. You need a deep and extensive knowledge of your subject. You need to research exhaustively, and to write carefully.

Michael Holroyd has already spent twelve years on his biography of George Bernard Shaw. He has a well-known subject, but he adds to the appeal of the book by considering every aspect of the writing meticulously:

> I think biography has grown and developed enormously during the course of the century, and I believe it's quite an exciting genre now, whereas in the past it was rather staid and really something that underpinned the status quo. Now it attempts to rewrite the past, and by doing that set the future on a different course. Now that's quite exciting. It has future applications, I think. Also we've learned an enormous amount from novelists – how to tell a story. I read thrillers because I want to structure the book so I can leave a chapter or a section in a particular place where readers want to know what's going to happen next.

International appeal

International appeal never hurt any writer, but it's particularly vital for non-fiction writers of illustrated books. Many of these books can only viably be published if they achieve large sales. Most package publishers try to sell their books worldwide (in different language editions, with the same pictures and the text translated) and naturally they look for book proposals that make this a realistic proposition. It's important to avoid a Little England – or a Little Anywhere – mentality. Geographical examples in your text should be spread as widely as possible; reference material should be as widely applicable as possible.

The title

If your publishers don't like your title, they will probably ask you to think of a new one – or suggest one to you. Listen to their advice, and think hard. Good titles sell books. The best ones are short, evocative and memorable. The fiction titles at the top of the 1988 bestseller list (*Rage, Savage, Hot Money, Destiny, Sepulchre, Misery*) prove this.

You may like to ponder the experiences of prolific (pseudonymous) romance writer John Marsh (quoted in *The Author*, Summer 1987). He analysed the Public Lending Right returns of his 80 registered novels, and found that books with titles containing the words 'doctor' or 'nurse' were twice as popular as those without. Next – in order – came 'love', 'romance' and 'marriage'.

Selling

However good – or formulaic – your book, readers won't buy it unless booksellers stock it. Booksellers won't stock it unless the publisher persuades them it's going to sell in large quantities. Publishers try to do this for all their books, but they try hardest for those they expect and need to sell in large quantities – that is, their lead titles.

If your book is a publisher's lead title (particularly a large paperback house's lead title) its odds of becoming a bestseller will be reasonably short. If it's at the bottom of the publisher's list, the odds will be almost infinitely long. Moral: if you want this book (not your next, or your tenth, but this very one) to be a bestseller, then you must hold out for a big advance and a place at the top of the list.

CHAPTER 10
Producing a typescript

You must have your manuscript typed or printed out before you submit it to a publisher. Few publishers will look at handwritten manuscripts, and even those who do (Mills & Boon, for example, are prepared to) much prefer typewritten ones.

The only exception is if your publisher asks for (and you agree to provide) text on computer floppy discs. Even then, it's usual also to provide a print-out.

How many copies?

If submitting an unsolicited typescript, one copy is sufficient. This should be an original, not a photocopy, unless it's so good that you can't tell the difference. Keep a copy yourself, in case the one you send out is lost, and for reference should the publisher come back to you with comments. Yours can be a photocopy or carbon. You may like to take a second carbon copy, in case the publisher requests a second copy on acceptance (as publishers sometimes do).

Carbons are cheaper than photocopies: typewriters and many computer printers will produce them. (You can use single-sheet carbon paper successfully in many printers. Multiple sets of continuous stationery are less fuss, but they cost more.) Note any top-copy handwritten alterations on the carbon, correct any typing mistakes clearly, and change the carbon paper well before the copies become illegible.

Your agent, if you have one, will want a file copy. S/he may need several more to send to foreign agents or publishers. Sometimes carbons are acceptable: ask.

If your book is commissioned, the number of copies required may be specified in your contract. Deliver that number: they will all be needed for different purposes. One top copy plus legible carbons should be acceptable.

It's expensive to produce photocopies of a long typescript. If you don't own a photocopier, try to negotiate a cheap deal with somebody who does. Ask a printer for a bulk discount. Ask at your place of work, school or university. Try to avoid high street bureaux, which are not cheap. If you can't get a reasonable deal locally, ask your agent or publisher. They may agree to make the copies for you at cost price. If buying a photocopier, avoid the very cheap, slow and messy ones, and check on the price of consumables.

Word processors enable you to run off multiple copies, but this can take a long time on a slow printer. Allow too for the cost of printer ribbons. Carbon copies are generally cheaper than multiple top copies from one-pass carbon ribbons.

Paper

Produce all copies, including your own copy, on A4 paper of reasonable (bond) weight. Bank (copy) paper will not do, and thicker paper will only make the typescript bulkier and more expensive to post.

Plain copier paper (not the heat-treated kind) is both acceptable and cheap. So is plain continuous computer stationery, so long as you remove the perforations and *separate the pages*. Buy in bulk, from a wholesaler or specialist office stationer. Don't buy small packs of typing paper from the newsagent round the corner: it will cost you far more.

Print quality

If your typewriter or printer uses multiple-pass ribbons, do start with a new, or nearly new, one, and change it if the print fades noticeably. Faint print does not tempt readers to persevere. Nor does dot-matrix print. Avoid any but the near-letter-quality kind.

If your computer printer produces poor quality output, see

if you can borrow a different one, or have your work printed out by a word processing bureau. This is a good argument for using a popular model of word processor: you'll have more trouble finding a bureau to handle discs with an unusual format.

Layout

Every publisher has their own 'house style', and many publishers produce detailed guidelines (some run to 20 pages or more) on typescripts, covering layout, preferred spellings, handling of footnotes and endnotes and other topics. If you have been commissioned by a publisher, or are writing with one publisher in mind, then you should obtain that publisher's guidelines, and follow them meticulously.

This is particularly necessary if you are producing a word-processed text that is to be typeset from your computer files, or text that will not be reprinted, but be reproduced exactly as you deliver it. You will also require special instructions if you are producing text for a highly illustrated book with complex page layouts.

The layout guidance I give here is second-best to any such detailed guidelines. If you follow it you will, however, produce the kind of typescript that will be acceptable to almost any publisher for a predominantly textual book. More detailed guidance is available in *Hart's Rules for Compositors and Readers* (OUP) and in *The Oxford Dictionary for Writers and Editors*, both of which I recommend for your reference library.

You should use one side of the paper only.

Leave wide margins on all four sides of the text. 1½" (40mm) is an accepted minimum; some writers like to leave 2" (50mm) margins. The Macmillan Press suggest 1" (25mm) minimum at the head, foot and right of the page, and 1½" (40mm) at the left.

Authors fretting over their paper bills are often tempted to reduce these margins. Do not. The space is needed by the copy editor and the printer's estimator. You may need to make annotations in it yourself, and it will protect your text if the typescript becomes battered.

Number the pages of your typescript consecutively. Do not

number every chapter individually (i.e., 1.1, 2.1 and so on) unless on specific instruction from the publisher. You may (and may be asked to) number preliminary sheets (e.g. title page, tables of contents, dedications) separately, in roman numerals, in which case page 1 will be the first page of the body of the text. It is normal to continue the main page numbering through all endmatter – that is, appendices, index and so on.

Number each page in the top right-hand corner, for quick visibility when flicking through. The number should be part of a standard header on all sheets, which gives your name (or pseudonym), the name of the book, which can be abbreviated to one or two words, and the page number. For example:

Cook   Tiger's Tail   123

Leave a space both above and below this header.

Every page of your typescript should be double-spaced: that is, with one full blank line (not a half line) in-between every line of type. This includes tables of contents, quotations, notes, appendices, tables, bibliographies, etc. It is immaterial how you expect any of this material to be laid out in the completed book.

Your copy editor will select typestyles and sizes for all your text, including headings and subheadings. Do not anticipate their choice by printing these – or quotations, notes, etc. – in unusual sizes or styles. If you have strong preferences on these matters, you can indicate them in a covering letter.

Stick to a standard ten or twelve pitch for everything (except, arguably, for a cover page, if you want the typescript to stand out from the mass), even if your printer can do all sorts of fancy flourishes. If possible, choose a typeface with a standard character spacing, not a proportional typeface, and do not justify the text (i.e. spread characters so that both right and left margins are aligned).

Do not use an italic-style, mock-handwriting or other fancy typeface for any of the text. Italics in the text are indicated by a single underline. This is one of the printers' mark-up conventions with which you will need to be familiar, most notably when correcting your proofs. There's a list in the *Writers' and Artists' Yearbook*; or see *Hart's Rules*, or ask your publisher.

Headings and divisions

Begin each new chapter on a fresh sheet of paper. Don't use a fresh sheet for subheadings within chapters: this will only make it hard for you and the publisher to calculate the overall length.

Most publishers prefer reasonably short chapter titles. If you have a long title, you may need to provide a short version for use in page headings. There's no standard convention for chapter numbering, though many publishers have preferred or required forms. Mills & Boon like chapter headings to be in capitals, centred, with the number (never a title) spelled out in full, like this:

CHAPTER ONE

while many academic publishers prefer arabic numerals, lower case and left-alignment:

Chapter 1
Introducing the Amiga Computer

Do not italicize or underline headings. However, you do need to show that headings are headings, and to mark the various ranks of subheadings, if any.

Single-level headings are easily and sufficiently indicated by a blank line above and below. For ranked headings, either use a numbering scheme (e.g. 1.2.4, 1.2.5) within the text, or mark the level (e.g. A, B and C) in the margin (and provide a key, if this does not seem to you self-explanatory).

Most publishers prefer you not to leave a blank space in-between text paragraphs, as this makes it harder to estimate the overall word-count. (Alas, this has never been explained to some writers of word processing programs.) Indicate a new paragraph by indenting the first word. This is not necessary after a heading or subheading.

Mark a break in the text that is not followed by a heading by leaving a double line space. Do not indent the paragraph that follows. You do not need a row of asterisks or dashes. If the break coincides with the bottom of a page you may need to make an additional note in the margin.

Alterations to the typescript

Alterations look messy and unprofessional. A small quantity are acceptable, but not a large quantity. If the level goes much above one per page, have the typescript redone.

Any short (one or two word) last-minute additions can be written (legibly) or typed within the body of the text. Make an insertion mark (⋏) in the line of text, and write clearly above. Do not write vertically in the margins. If you need to make a large insertion, write 'see sheet xxx.a' and type the insertion on a separate *full-sized* sheet.

Inserted sheets are normally numbered a, b, c, etc. If pages 175a and 175b follow 175, note under the page number of 175, '175a follows'. On 175a, note '175b follows'; on 175b, '176 follows'. Omitted sheets are marked similarly: for example, on 175, 'No pp. 176 to 180. 181 follows.' If this happens every few pages, then renumber (or retype) the entire typescript.

Some authors 'cut and paste' their typescripts when they need to make larger-scale changes. This is acceptable so long as you do it neatly and in moderation. Your cut-and-pasted sheets should always end up A4-sized. Though glue is acceptable so long as the end resuit is not sticky, it is less satisfactory to use staples, pins, clips and Sellotape. Photocopying cut-and-pasted sheets is a good technique. Retyping is a better solution – and easily achieved if you have a word processor.

Book matter

There's no set rule about what your typescript should contain: it depends what type of book you produce. It may include any or all of these:

- *A cover sheet* (optional). If you want to produce a fancy cover sheet in order to make your typescript stand out, it should be *in addition to* the conventional title page.
- *A title page* (always required), typed in standard font. This will list:
  * The title in full, plus any subtitle.
  * The author's name, exactly as it is to appear on the book. If you plan to use a pseudonym, use this and not your real name.

* The number of pages in the typescript.
* An approximate word count (optional).
* A note of the copyright holder, if it is not you personally (e.g. if you are assigning copyright to a limited company). Otherwise, this is optional.
* (optional) The rights you are offering, especially if these are restricted – e.g. British volume rights, world English language volume rights. Note that you must offer a book publisher volume rights; serial rights are what you offer to a newspaper or magazine.

The title page will look something like this:

Savage Passion

by

Sally Cook

Copyright 1990 SC Enterprises Ltd.

227 pages typescript
Approx. 52,000 words

British volume rights offered

Either here or at the head of the first page of text, indicate your full name (real, not pseudonym), address, and daytime telephone number. If you have an agent, give their name, address and telephone number, too.

- *Preliminary pages* (optional). The publisher normally sets out the prelims in a standard format. You need not worry about copyright statements, half-titles, ISBN numbers and the like. But if you want to see any of the following in the finished book, you will need to provide the necessary text:
  * A list of your other publications. The usual style is to give only the title and name of any co-author(s).
  * A dedication.
  * A foreword (written by somebody other than yourself). Sometimes publishers arrange for this to be written; sometimes authors arrange it.
  * An introduction or preface (written by you as author

or editor). Prefaces generally end with the author's name or initials, and the date; some authors mention a location, too. For example:

Mary Bloggs
Santander, Spain
July 1988

* Acknowledgements for help received, if not included in the preface.
* Acknowledgements for copyright permission, if you have quoted copyright text or used copyright illustrations (occasionally printed as endmatter).
* A list of abbreviations, if required in a specialist book (again, sometimes printed as endmatter).
* A brief biography of yourself, if required. This appears as part of the prelims in, for example, Pelican originals.
* Notes on contributors, if you are the editor of a book comprising several separate contributions (also sometimes printed as endmatter).

- *A table of contents*. Not usual for fiction, even where there are parts or chapters. Normally required for non-fiction.

  List the level of detail you would prefer, though the editor may overrule you.

  The typescript page numbering will differ from the printed page numbering, but write it in, in pencil, as an aid to the editor.

  Include all endmatter (see below).

- *A list of tables* (if any). Tables should be clearly distinguished from line illustrations. Each table should be typed on a separate sheet, and the sheets collated at the back of the typescript, not interleaved with the main body of the text. Indicate clearly in the margin of the text where the table should ideally be placed. Number the tables clearly, and provide a list of numbers, headings and (typescript) page number references.

- *A list of illustrations* (if any). Old-fashioned typesetting methods made a strict distinction between line, half-tone and plate (i.e. photographic) illustrations. Each required a different handling method. With modern printing methods this distinction is less vital, and typically a whole page, which may contain text and a variety of illustrations, is made up and printed in one operation. But you must still keep illustrations separate from the body of the typescript, unless you have clear instructions to the contrary.

Details on how to deliver illustrations are given later in the chapter. Each one must be numbered, whether or not the numbers are to appear in the book. Your list should give the illustration numbers, brief captions or, if your captions are long, a brief description of each illustration (for the editor's reference – this may not appear in the book itself) and typescript page references. Cross-reference with marginal notes in the typescript.

Captions, whether included here or not, should be typed on separate sheets of paper, clearly numbered, and collated at the back of the typescript.

Indicate which illustrations you are enclosing; which you have available, but are not enclosing; which you hope to obtain but do not yet have, or do not yet have permission to use. Indicate whether you are enclosing roughs or finished artwork. It is not advisable to spend time and money on having finished artwork prepared, searching for pictures or obtaining permission, before you have a contract for the book.

If you are submitting unsolicited material requiring a great many illustrations, enclose only a few samples, and do not send anything that is irreplaceable. An editor should be able to gauge the general quality from good photocopies. If you feel you must send precious originals, consult the editor first.

- *The body of the text*. Do not include footnotes except by prior agreement: they are expensive to produce, and endnotes are now far more common. You can list these either at the end of each chapter, or at the end of the body of text, as you prefer, or as your editor directs.

- *Endmatter* (optional). Depending on the type of book, this may include any or all of the following:
  * one or more appendices;

* endnotes, suitably numbered for reference;
* a glossary;
* a bibliography;
* other reference material or acknowledgements as discussed under prelims above.

All of these should be numbered as continuations of the main text.

- *An index* (optional).
  Unless you know your book is to be phototypeset direct from your typescript, you will not yet be in a position to provide a final index. Some writers start preparing an index when they deliver the typescript, but many leave it until the proof stage.
  You can if you wish indicate whether you think an index is required, and whether you are willing to prepare one yourself. (If not, you may have to pay part or all of the fee of a professional indexer.)
- *At the very end of the typescript, note 'the end'*. This won't appear in the book, but it is helpful to the editor.

Overall presentation

Generally publishers do not like typescripts to be fastened together in sections with staples, paperclips or tags, hole-punched and put in ring binders, or bound in any form.

What's left? You collate the pages neatly, put a blank sheet of paper (or thin sheet of cardboard) at the front and back, and secure with elastic bands. If your blank paper came in a cardboard box, you can put the bundle into this. Pack carefully, and post.

True, it sounds flimsy, but publishers are used to handling typescripts in this form. It isn't risky so long as you number every sheet, and mark every sheet with your name and the title.

Typing services

There is no shortage of home typists and word processor

operators who are able and willing to type manuscripts. Many of them advertise in local papers and in specialist writers' magazines. Those who advertise in *The Author* all have to provide references: if you obtain an unfamiliar typist from another source, check on his or her quality of work before contracting out your entire manuscript.

If you expect to produce more than one draft, use a word processor operator.

If you receive layout instructions from your publisher, ensure that you pass them on to your typist.

Disk files

Submitting material on floppy discs can be a real winner. It's cheaper to mail discs than typescripts. (Mail them in the conventional way, in special disc folders: electronic mail comes much more expensive for high volumes of material.) You don't have to spend hours (and money) turning out multiple hard copies of your masterpiece, and typesetting direct from disc files is faster, cheaper and more error-free than rekeying.

There are a few possible drawbacks for the author, though. Not all computers can produce or read all disc files, and incompatibility problems can be a major headache. Check at an early stage (before buying a word processor, if you do not already have one) whether your format will be acceptable.

You may be asked to create files in a format that your word processor does not support. You may be asked to key in complex sequences of typesetting commands. Before agreeing to this, ensure that you will be able to produce exactly what you undertake to produce. Ensure that you understand how much work will be involved. If it will mean a lot of additional work, or additional expense, point this out – and ask to be paid or reimbursed.

It's best, while working on the text and when submitting it, to create, not one incredibly long disc file, but a series of moderate-sized files: say, of single-chapter length, or a maximum of around 10,000 words. Give them self-explanatory names (for example CHAPTER.1, and CHAPTER.2) and list these on the disc label, together with the book title and author's name.

You should, of course, keep duplicate discs (and backups of your duplicates) and I advise you to keep a hard copy of the text as well, for additional security.

Illustrations

It is not as expensive as it used to be to print line and half-tone illustrations, but it can still be very expensive to create them in the first place. If your book will require illustrations, you should discuss how they will be produced (and who will pay the bills) before the contract is signed.

Colour printing is still much more expensive than grey-tone, and publishers will generally only agree to it when they are confident of comparatively large sales. It is also very expensive nowadays to produce folded inset maps and the like, and these should be avoided wherever possible.

If you can produce the illustrations yourself, the publisher will naturally be relieved - so long as your work is of a suitable standard. If you cannot, you will be expected to produce roughs from which the illustrator can work. Illustrators cannot read minds, so your roughs must be clear, and contain all the necessary information.

Sometimes the author produces sketches but not lettering, which is added by a professional. The best way to handle this is to do the drawing and then photocopy it. You write in rough on the photocopy, and the pro works on the original.

Ideally you should draw your illustrations larger than the size they are to be printed, and scale all of them up by the same proportion, so they can be photoreduced in a batch. Double size is often ideal. Bear in mind the page size (ask the publisher if in doubt) and try to avoid landscape illustrations (that is, ones for which you have to turn the book sideways). It's important to use good black ink.

If you plan to provide photographs, they should be clear ones, and wherever possible you should provide black and white prints where they are to be reproduced in black and white.

If part of a photo is to be masked out, or you want a caption or other markings to be printed over it, then indicate your instructions on an overlay. Fold a sheet of thin paper over the photo, fasten it to the back with adhesive tape, and mark your requirements on this. Be careful to avoid marking or denting the photo.

Both photographs and drawings must be clearly marked. The best way to do this with photographs is to write out a label in ink and then stick it on the back.

Enclose original artwork of any kind in one or more envelopes, which again should be clearly marked. It's a good idea to put in the envelope a copy of the list of illustrations that (following the instructions above) you included with the typescript. The illustrations should be sorted into the order in which they will appear in the book. If there are many, you may find it helpful to use a separate envelope for each chapter or major section of the book.

Picture libraries

If you want to use photographs in your book, but you do not possess suitable ones, you may be able to obtain them from a picture library. These are repositories of good quality photographs: you pay for the use of those you require. There's a list of picture libraries in the *Writers' and Artists' Yearbook*, with a note of their specialities.

Though picture libraries index their holdings thoroughly, finding the right picture can still be a complex business. If you do not have the time or expertise to do it yourself, you can (at a price) hire a specialist picture researcher.

Ian McLachlan resorted to picture libraries when he was locating illustrations for his book on aircraft recovery, *Final Flights*. He wanted to use as many as possible of his own photographs, feeling that the specialist audience at whom the book is largely aimed would not appreciate finding the book to be crammed with pictures they might already have copies of in other books, but he needed to supplement his own holdings with existing good-quality photographs of the planes he discusses.

Photographer John Hedgecoe's experience is rather different:

> I'd prefer in a way to shoot everything new, but publishers actually like a percentage of known pictures to go in a

book, because they think it gives some sort of continuity.

If you are hired as a writer by a publisher of highly illustrated books, particularly a package publisher, then you may find that the publisher takes full responsibility for illustrations. Not only will you not be expected to locate the illustrations yourself, you may not even see them until the book is published.

CHAPTER 11
After delivery

Your publishers may receive your final typescript either before or after they have firmly undertaken to publish your book. In either case, once it is received it will be read through by an editor.

Editor's titles vary, but this one may be called something like 'commissioning editor', to distinguish him or her from the 'copy editor' whose task is to prepare the typescript for the printer. (In small publishing houses one person may do both these tasks.) This is the editor who will normally act as a contact point for you as author. The typescript may also go to an outside reader for comments.

If the editor feels that the book requires major changes, or finds any parts of it to be unclear, s/he will tell you so at this stage, and probably return the typescript so that you can amend it. Publishers should not, and generally do not, substantially alter a typescript without consulting the author.

When (sometimes before) you and the editor have agreed the overall contents, the publisher should schedule the remaining stages in getting the book published. Often they will tell you – and if they don't, you can ask them – when you will be expected to correct the proofs, and what the publication date will be.

Next, the typescript will (assuming the book is conventionally edited and printed) pass on to the copy editing stage. The copy editor will raise small queries over the phrasing and contents with you. S/he checks for consistency, and should notice, for instance, if your character's eyes change from blue to grey halfway through the book. S/he often makes smaller changes without referring to you: correcting spelling and punctuation, and rephrasing anything s/he considers to be confusingly or clumsily expressed.

Some copy editors rewrite virtually every sentence, while others make few, or no, changes to typescripts. Which they do depends as much on their style of working as on your writing ability.

Journalists are used to having this type of change made without consultation, but most authors prefer to have, and many insist on having, an opportunity to vet the alterations. It's advisable to ask to see a copy of the edited manuscript. Though you will see the amended version when you are sent the proofs, you will be much more popular if you make alterations before the text goes to the printers.

You may be sent the entire marked-up typescript, or you may just receive a list of queries and proposed amendments. The latter is less satisfactory, because it often doesn't indicate omitted commas and the like.

At the same time, the production department will be at work designing your book, organizing and scheduling the printing, jacket design, binding and so on.

Next the book is sent to the printers. Once the text is keyed in and laid out, you will be sent the proofs for correction. This is usual even if the book is typeset from your original discs, since you may need to comment on the typestyles or page layout.

Normally nowadays you will see *page proofs*, which reproduce (sometimes at a different size) each page of the finished book. You are generally expected to read these through and to correct errors in them: miskeyings, omitted paragraphs, misunderstandings over headings, etc. You will also fill in missing page references, and compile the index if one is required.

Often the publishers will also have the proofs read, and your corrections will be collated with those discovered by the other reader. A few publishers, including Mills & Boon, rely primarily on in-house proofreading: their authors receive proofs, but are not compelled to correct them.

Though authors are permitted to make the occasional small alteration to their text at proof stage, this is not a stage at which you can have large-scale second thoughts about your content. Corrections are expensive to implement, especially if they disturb the layout of more than one page. If you make too many corrections (other than of printer's errors) you may be charged for them.

You will probably also be asked to complete a marketing questionnaire, with details for the sales force and publicity department of the market for your book, media contacts who may help promote it, suggestions for where review copies should be sent, and so on.

Typically books are published approximately a year after the final typescript is agreed. Bound copies are available – and you can expect to receive your author's free copies – about a month beforehand.

Most first books receive only a little publicity: you are more likely to be offered a ten-minute interview on your local radio station than an appearance on a networked TV chat show. Author tours and signing sessions are generally reserved for established names, and only a very small minority of book launches are celebrated with a launch party.

Major revisions

Few authors welcome it when a publisher asks for drastic alterations to their text, but many bring themselves to accept it, particularly when they judge that the prospects of getting the book accepted unrevised by another publisher are not good. Some even confess that the suggested changes improve the book, but others harbour lasting regrets.

Don't rush into a decision to accept substantial cuts or alterations. You will almost always be granted time to consider if you ask for it. If you want to try offering the book elsewhere, do say so: it's understandable that you should, and many publishers will leave their offer open for several months while you do so.

During the last war, Jean Rennie was told about seven child stowaways who had taken a ship from Greenock (her home town) in 1868. Several years later she decided to write a novel about this incident. Her ideas expanded during the research and writing, until she produced a saga which began in 1847 and ended in 1952.

She spent twenty years searching for a publisher for this book, which she called *World Enough for Me*. Finally, in 1987, her agent rang to say that William Kimber were interested in publishing it – but only after revision. Kimber wanted to cut the book, and to make it focus not on the stowaways, but on the heroine who married the brutal first mate of the ship involved in the incident.

Rennie was then 81: she couldn't realistically pass up this long-awaited offer. The book, her first novel, was duly published with a new title, *A Prouder Music*, and a plot from which almost all mention of the stowaways had been removed. But her regret persists, and she still says, 'If they ever do a reprint, I'm going to say I want it published in its entirety with the story of the stowaways in it.'

Janet Hutcheon had a similar experience with her first novel, published by Robert Hale:

> It has a relationship in it which ends up happily, but I didn't see it as a romance, more as a psychological suspense type of thing. They wanted to have it as long as I cut it down to size, and I did this by cutting out the subplot which I thought decimated the book and turned it into something rather more ordinary.

Small alterations

Even trivial changes can deeply upset authors who take great care with their typescripts. Don't assume that none will be made: ask to see the copy-edited text. If you object to any of the changes that have been made, say so. The publishers will often back down.

Historical biographer Jasper Ridley:

> The text of *John Knox* was passed to a copy editor, and when the proofs came I saw that this wretched copy editor had completely rewritten my book, in a most atrocious style. For example, where I said, "The Queen hated Albany, and Albany hated the Queen," this copy editor had changed it to, "The Queen hated Albany, and the latter reciprocated the feelings of the former."
>
> I said, we can't have that, and the OUP were very apologetic. They redid the whole thing.

Robert Short, co-author of a book on surrealist artist Hans Bellmer:

We had the most outrageous changes made. It really sent me reeling. What I thought was complicated wording which was necessary to the complexity of the ideas was simplified into a kind of banal English by our editor at Quartet. But when we actually confronted her and said look, there is a reason for this turn of phrase and that turn of phrase, she sort of caved in and the book ended up just like we wanted it.

Proofreading

This is a chore, but don't skimp it. Careless slips in a book can mar readers' enjoyment, or render it useless for reference purposes. Use the standard proof marks (a list can be found in the *Writers' and Artists' Yearbook* and elsewhere, or ask your publisher) and two colours of ink: red for correcting printer's errors, and black or blue for your own alterations.

Ensure that you mark all changes clearly in the margins. The printer only looks there, and changes in the body of the text that are not flagged will not be noticed.

Check on all the following:

- All blank or dummy page references should be completed. Complete the page references in the contents list if this has not already been done.
- Ensure that illustrations are set in the right places, are numbered correctly, and that references to them in the text are correct.
- Check that no passages are missing or repeated.
- Check that running headlines (if used) are correct, and present on every page.
- Check the chapter titles on the contents page against those in the text.

If you find it necessary to insert or delete passages of more than one line, particularly if these are your own second thoughts, not printer's errors, try to balance these with other insertions or deletions so that a minimum of text will have to be reset.

Indexing

This too is a chore, but an important one. Word processing 'index' programs are of little help: one, because the page divisions in the proofs will differ from those in your typescript, and two, because few of them handle analytical indexes, as opposed to the mechanical every-entry-of-significant-words type, which is far less satisfactory.

It's not easy for beginners to judge how long an index will turn out. Generally your publisher will accept whatever length you come up with within reason, but sometimes s/he may ask for an index of a specific length. It's most practicable to work through the proofs indexing as you think preferable, then edit afterwards to bring it to the right length.

Indexing methods vary. Some authors like to start by marking on the typescript (by underlining or highlighting) all words and phrases to be included, but unless you expect to be very pressed for time, it's less work to wait until the proofs arrive.

For a short index, it's sufficient to mark sheets of paper with letters of the alphabet, and to make entries on each as you come across them. You can then sort each sheet into alphabetical order when it comes to typing up. Longer indexes are better handled on index cards, one for each entry – or sometimes more than one, if you will need several subentries.

There's no fixed rule for layout, particularly where there are lots of sub-entries. Ask your publisher, or use any method that seems to you to be clear.

If you need advice on indexing, there's a good short guide produced by the Cambridge Univeristy Press (see Bibliography). Indexes, too, need proofreading, but this is usually handled in-house by the publisher.

CHAPTER 12
The business

When you start to consider writing for publication, you are embarking on a business venture. Even if you don't see it that way, the Inland Revenue will. Being business-like from the start will not only increase your chances of publication, it will also save you money and headaches if and when your book is accepted.

Self-employment

If you are writing books (or articles, poems or short stories) for publication other than in the course of your paid employment, then you are, for this purpose, self-employed. It's important that you tell your Tax Inspector and the Department of Health and Social Security, who deal with National Insurance contributions (or the equivalent bodies in your home country) of this, whether or not you are also in paid employment. You should do this immediately you start, even if there is as yet no publisher in sight for your work. The Inland Revenue don't only tax your income, they also give you credit for your expenses.

Self-employed people are normally obliged to pay National Insurance contributions, but if your expected earnings are very low (or zero) then you can apply for exemption from these.

You must declare all income, however small and casual, and once you exceed the taxation limits you will, of course, have to pay income tax.

I cannot outline the relevant legislation in detail here. Your tax office and DSS office will advise you, or you may prefer to consult an accountant or other financial adviser.

It is a basic requirement that you maintain (and keep for several years) adequate records from which your income and expenditure can be calculated.

Expenses

Whatever you write, you will incur expenses. At the very least, you'll use up paper, pens, typewriter or printer ribbons, envelopes and other stationery items. You will post letters and make telephone calls; you may travel, for research (even a trip to the local library counts) or to consult an editor or agent.

You will acquire reference books, and you may subscribe to specialist magazines. You will light and heat your workplace, and use electricity to power your computer. You may need to employ a researcher or a typist. You may join the Society of Authors or another trade organization.

If you have previously been writing as a hobby, with no expectation of publication, it may not immediately be obvious to you that these are all legitimate business expenses which you can (subject to Inland Revenue approval) set off against your income – including your income from sources other than writing. But if you're writing with a reasonable expectation of publication, you are involved in a business venture, and this is the case. If and when you do receive income from your writing, the Inland Revenue won't waste any time in taxing you on that!

It is of course necessary for you to convince the Inland Revenue that your writing is more than just an expensive hobby. The more business-like the manner in which you go about it, the more chance you have of doing this. It's not necessary to produce a contract for your book, so long as you can prove (for example, by showing the tax office carbons of your letters to publishers and agents) that you are making serious efforts to sell it.

It's also necessary for you to keep records of the equipment that you acquire for use in your business, as this may attract capital allowances. Your 'plant and machinery' may include a car, a typewriter, a computer or word processor, a printer, a photocopier, office furniture, a telephone answering machine, and your reference library. If you buy something that will help with your writing, and that you would not otherwise be buying, then you should tell your accountant or tax office. You'll lose nothing if they disallow it, and gain if they allow it as capital expenditure.

Records

For your own and for legal purposes, you should keep full records of all your writing-related activity. These should include:

- Accounts of all your income and expenditure, in a clear and organized form, together with receipts, invoices, advice notes, etc.
- Copies of all letters you write. If you habitually phone rather than write, you may find it helpful to log phone calls.
- If you send out a variety of work (articles to magazines, a string of romances to publishers), a log of what you sent to whom, and when – so that you can follow up after a reasonable interval has passed.
- Contact and client name and address lists. (If you put these onto a computer, you may become liable to register under the Data Protection Act.)
- Copies of everything you have written.
- Copies of everything you have had published.
- If you exceed the VAT registration limits (see below), VAT records in the prescribed form.

Money handling

It's not essential to use an accountant if your expected income is very small. However, a good accountant may well save you several times more than his fee, by pointing out to you expenses that you have failed to claim, and helping you order your financial affairs to your best advantage.

It's not essential that you maintain a separate business bank account, so long as you keep detailed records of all business-related financial transactions.

It is essential that you prepare accounts for your writing activity on an annual basis. It is up to you to decide when your financial year will begin and end. There's currently an advantage in the UK in ending your financial year just after the end of the tax year (that is, on or around the end of April) as this will maximize your time lag before you have to pay tax on your earnings.

Your income as a writer will probably be spasmodic, and may vary drastically from year to year. If you expect to receive a very large single payment, you may be able to 'spread' it for income tax purposes over several years. There is no substitute in these circumstances for proper professional advice.

Grants, allowances and prizes

At the time of writing, the British Government operates an Enterprise Allowance scheme which provides financial help to individuals setting up small businesses. There's no guarantee that the Enterprise Allowance scheme will last indefinitely, but if you hope to make writing your major source of income you should certainly enquire whether you would be eligible for a grant or allowance to help you get established.

Jan Palmer, a writer and illustrator, obtained an Enterprise Allowance. She was expected to invest £1,000 in her enterprise (which she spent on a word processing system), and she received a basic income of £40 per week for a year, which she spent trying to write romances for Mills & Boon. Though Palmer received some encouraging feedback from Mills & Boon, she wasn't successful in selling any romances within the year. However, this did not affect her allowance she received, she regarded the year as 'a training period', and it has left her in a better position to continue than she would have been had she not had the allowance.

Regional arts associations and other arts-oriented organizations make grants from time to time to aspiring writers, and there are a number of literary prizes (some worth several thousands of pounds) which are open to unpublished writers. As an unpublished writer, it is up to you to find out about and apply for these. Many of these are listed in the *Writers' and Artists' Yearbook* and *The Writer's Handbook*.

VAT registration

Though books themselves do not (at the time of writing) incur Value Added Tax in the UK, VAT *is* payable on royalties and advances to authors, agents' fees, stationery, and most capital equipment.

Self-employed writing counts as a business enterprise for VAT purposes, and any writer whose income (from this and other business activities) exceeds the registration limits must register for VAT. The limits are regularly increased broadly in line with inflation, but currently (1989) stand at £22,100 per year, or £7,500 in any one quarter. You must register as soon as you have reason to expect your income to exceed the limits: do not wait until it actually does so. Writers whose income is below these limits can apply for voluntary registration.

Registration is actually a bonus for most writers. You will need to fill in a form and make a payment every three months, but publishers normally pay VAT without quibbling on top of your normal advance or royalty figure, and you can deduct VAT from all your outgoings. So your paper, pens, etc. and your agent's fees will cost you (currently) 15 per cent less than if you are unregistered; and you should find that there's normally a surplus in your VAT fund, on which you can collect interest for up to four months before you have to pay it over.

Public Lending Right

Once you have a book published, you can register for Public

Lending Right (PLR). Books are not automatically registered for PLR on publication: you must apply to be registered, and must notify the PLR Office of each new book (and new edition of a book, if it is given a different ISBN) that you have published. The address of the British PLR Office is given in the Appendix.

The number of loans of any title nationwide is estimated, from actual loan data taken from a sample of libraries. The rate of PLR per notional library loan currently (for the period July 1987 to June 1988) stands at 1.45p. You may justifiably think this is a trivial sum, but when multiplied by the estimated number of loans it can mount up very satisfactorily. The maximum payment to any author is currently £6,000, and 67 authors received this amount for the year to June 1988, though 8,854 authors received less than £100, and sadly 2,823 authors received nothing at all.

The Authors' Licensing and Collecting Society handles payments of German Public Lending Right, and may in future handle other rights payments; it is worth while registering your interests with this Society, especially if your book may be available in German libraries.

Trade associations

Writers in the UK have two main trade associations: The Writers' Guild, which is affiliated to the TUC, and The Society of Authors, which is independent. The Writers' Guild was initially called the Screenwriters' Guild, and though book authors subsequently became eligible for full membership, it is still oriented towards a wider range of media coverage than The Society of Authors.

Both organizations do valuable work on behalf of authors generally (for example, campaigning for PLR, and now for Minimum Terms Agreements with publishers), and both provide help and advice to members. Newsletters, conferences and so on help to keep authors in touch with each other, and up to date with developments that may affect their work. It is not necessary to be a full-time author in order to join, and membership is open to those who have just been offered a first contract for publication.

I strongly advise you to join one or both organizations once you become eligible to do so. Their addresses are listed in the Appendix.

There are also a great many more specialist writers' organizations, details of which are given in *The Writer's Handbook* and (more extensively) in the *Writers' and Artists' Yearbook*. A special mention, too, for PEN, a world-wide association of writers which (among other things) campaigns for freedom of expression, and works on behalf of imprisoned writers.

Writing full time

Being published does get easier after you've made the first breakthrough, but not much easier. Each book you write has to be sold on its own merits: publishers rarely pay retainers to authors, or contract to publish more than a couple of books at a time by very well-established authors. 'Option' clauses in writers' contracts give publishers the opportunity, but not the obligation, to publish subsequent works.

Many long-standing authors still suffer rejections – if their work falls out of fashion, if they pick an unpopular subject, or if the publisher simply doesn't like their latest effort. Few books earn their authors a substantial amount of money, and the vast majority of published writers do not rely upon their writing to provide the bulk of their income.

Writing full time is at best a precarious business. It's all too easy for the full-time author to turn into a hack, producing too many books too quickly, with a bare minimum of research and revision, because of the financial pressure. Few full-time authors can afford the luxury of artistic experiment: most have to keep on producing what they already know is likely to sell.

There are other disadvantages, too, to writing full time. It's a lonely business, and isolating. Most people need the stimulation of fellow workers, and writers in particular constantly need to glean new subject matter. That isn't easy when you spend most of your days shut up in a back bedroom with just your word processor for company.

You may think I protest too much: after all, I do it myself

from choice. There are pluses, too. There's the freedom of being your own boss, and the luxury of having time to write when you're not already tired from a full day's work. There's the flexibility of having a job that you can do anywhere, any time – in the bath, in a remote holiday cottage, with the baby on your lap. Sometimes it's difficult to sustain the high level of motivation needed, but it's never boring.

Even so, I wouldn't recommend anyone to try writing full time on the strength of one, or even two, successful publications – and I would hesitate to recommend it to any fiction writer, however well established. Only a few very disciplined writers manage to keep producing saleable fiction year after year. For many more, the pressure of having to write to make a living can dry up the creative juices overnight. Whatever the drawbacks, there's much to be said for writing part, and not full time.

CHAPTER 13
Rejections

Almost every author receives rejections at some point. No author ever gets to like them, but the first sharp pain does dull with time, and successful authors persevere in spite of them.

Rejection letters

These are often painfully short and uninformative. In part this is because editors, readers and agents don't have the time to criticize unwanted typescripts in depth; in part it's because there are dangers in making specific criticisms. Most people whose work is abysmal prefer not to be told so in brutal terms, and people who are told, for instance, 'your characterization lets your novel down' might wrongly conclude that a little work on the characterization would quickly turn their effort into a bestseller, when this is far from being so.

Would-be authors sometimes spend hours mulling over the phrasing of even the most innocuous rejection. Don't read too much into formulae like 'not quite right for us' or 'our list is full'. There's usually no deep meaning behind them: the writer is only trying to find something polite to say without taking all morning over it. How friendly the letter is probably depends far more on the writer's mood that morning than on their opinion of your work.

Editor Patrick Janson-Smith of Transworld:

> I loathe rejecting books, and always try and write a polite word. But I find myself these days being more and more

> brutal, because I think sometimes a gentle rejection gives people false hopes.

Informative comments and suggestions – for instance, advice to try a specific alternative publisher, or a warning that your subject is insufficiently commercial – are usually meant to be helpful, and are probably right.

It's a hopeful sign if the publisher or agent asks to see your next novel; they won't normally ask to unless they detect a spark of promise in your work. It's a very hopeful sign if you do receive a long letter with detailed comments, particularly if you are invited to revise the work and resubmit it. Publishers do not go to this trouble unless there is a real possibility that they will accept a revised text, though naturally they will avoid saying anything that might be construed as a promise to do so.

Particularly if you're submitting a proposal for a non-fiction book, you may find that phoning to discuss it before submitting is more informative than merely writing. I don't advise you to phone and ask for an explanation after you've received a rejection.

How much of it was read?

Naturally, nobody will tell you this, and you'll rarely be able to deduce it from the rejection letter. If you really want to know, you can find out by doctoring the typescript. George Target:

> When I send a manuscript up I always doctor it. I use stamp hinges which I stick on the bottom left-hand corner at various places in the manuscript, so I know how far it's been read, because when you open the page it tears.

This and other methods aren't infallible, because different readers have different methods of skimming typescripts. Some read the first few pages; some read the ending; some read bits in the middle.

Be warned: the answer is often very little – perhaps only a page or two. This is depressing and frustrating, but neither pleas, tirades nor blackmail threats are likely to make the publisher go back and read more. If you try to find out how much has been read, do accept that you're doing so for your own information, and not so that you can grab the phone to complain. If you want to make the publisher read more, you've just got to make your typescript more lively, interesting, gripping, etc.

What to do after a rejection

It helps, especially with fiction, if you start writing your next book before you receive a verdict on the first. Don't wait until you get an acceptance: it could take years, and even if you get your book accepted immediately, the break will make it harder to get started again.

Unless you've received specific advice that leads you to rethink, submit the book to the next publisher on your list automatically. Don't shelve it and tell yourself that you'll do something with it in a month or two: keep going.

Romance writer Elizabeth Oldfield took this approach. She initially gave herself six months to make a success of writing romances. Her first typescript took her three months to write, and by the time Mills & Boon sent it back, saying encouragingly that they had liked it but felt not enough happened in the plot, she had almost finished the second story. Oldfield's first romance was accepted after a rewrite, but by then the one that she wrote second had already been accepted.

Novelist Kathy Page:

> I sent the first one off, and I'd already started another one. I thought, you hear all these stories so it's unlikely to get published. I'll just forget about it now and get on with the next one. So it was a sort of psychological management, not to get too wound up. I know people who write one and they end up hanging around forever because they won't write the next one until they find out what's happened to it.

It's up to you, and your fund of stamp money, how many publishers you try if you keep receiving rejections. I'd advise you to take a serious look at your submission after five or six rejections. Enough time will have gone by since you first prepared it for you to be able to look at it more objectively.

Often you'll see flaws that weren't apparent while you were writing or immediately afterwards, and will be able to set about improving it before resubmitting.

What did you do wrong?

There's no single answer. You might have been let down by insufficiently attractive subject matter, insufficiently impressive qualifications as author, failings in your presentation, obvious factual slips because of insufficient research, slipshod, unimaginative, convoluted or plodding prose, or any combination of these and similar failings.

One advantage of submitting a synopsis, not a complete typescript, for non-fiction is that you can be reasonably confident that the lack of appeal lies in your subject or presentation of it, and not in your literary style.

How can you put it right?

Naturally you will want to absorb and consider any comments you receive, and to review the material carefully yourself. This process may make it apparent where the major shortcoming lies.

If your research or your presentation has let you down, the only solution is to go back and do it more thoroughly and professionally.

It's particularly dispiriting if you are told that your proposed subject isn't saleable enough, but all may not be lost. Try asking yourself the following questions:

- Can you re-angle the book so that it will be of wider interest – for example, by focusing less on your own experiences, and including more practical advice?
- Can you widen or narrow your focus, so as to increase the market appeal or make it more obviously different from competing books?
- Have you done all that you can to sell the book – by describing it in lively terms, outlining its intended

audience accurately, pinpointing its particular market appeal?

If your literary style is your major failing, the answer is, of course, to revise your text. I discuss revision methods below.

However, it may not be apparent to you on a re-read why your brilliant novel or perfectly presented synopsis didn't grab the editor. In this case, assuming you want to persevere, you will need to find someone else who can suggest to you where its shortcomings may lie.

Feedback, expert and inexpert

Some writers show their work to friends and relations; others don't. Not all your friends and relations will have the knowledge and ability to assess your work accurately, most of them will probably hesitate to be frank about its limitations, and you yourself may well prefer to receive encouragement rather than criticism from your nearest and dearest.

Though amateurs may not be able to judge the market appeal of your book, they are often helpful in pointing out practical shortcomings. It's not easy for the beginning writer to appreciate how much people need to know in order to follow the story. Kathy Page:

> You can go off on a tangent for so long if you write without showing it to anyone. Completely convinced that what you're meaning is what you're saying, and oblivious to the fact that you might sometimes slightly be saying it but not really. Also completely oblivious to the fact that you might possibly expand it or say something more interesting, or that you keep using the same words fifty times all the way through. You're blind to your own work sometimes through reading it so much.

In many ways it is far better if you can get an expert opinion on your work, from somebody who is used to evaluating book proposals, and can be trusted to advise you honestly about yours.

If you employ an agent, they may perform this function for you. If you have contacts in publishing houses, you may be able to prevail upon one of them. If not, you may well find it worth while to join a writers' group or to go on a course for writers.

Some creative writing groups and writers' circles deal exclusively with 'literary' forms of writing – basically fiction, poetry and memoirs – but others deal with all types of writing, and a few specialize in non-fiction.

Any group tends to evolve its own style, and you may need to try several before you find one which meets your requirements. George Target, for instance, runs a course called *Writing for Pleasure and Profit* at Wensun Lodge in Norwich. He tends to stress the profit more than the pleasure, so his course caters largely for practical writers of magazine articles, short stories and general non-fiction.

Target has been running his course for about eight years:

> We start with around 90 in September and dwindle to three classes of 10 or 12 at the end of the year. Most of my course is about getting round editors, planting seedcorn and getting a response.
>
> Over the course of the years seven or eight students have had full-length books published, and no end of articles. It does work, like a brisk cold bath first thing in the morning. They're not literature but they are useful books for people: for example, on how to put up a set of shelves. This is not despicable information. If it makes their house a nicer place to live in, good. And how to cook a cake. What better than to have five or six kids at a party enjoying your cake? There's more good that comes from a cake recipe than from every novel that Martin Amis will ever write.

Target's own fiction hasn't always been perfectly tailored to the market-place, but he stresses marketability to his students, and has little time for what he calls 'twitching nostrils writing'. So his course wouldn't do for anyone who wanted to write 'frightfully homosexual short stories about fearful goings-on in cocktail bars', but it could suit a would-be romance writer very well:

> To be happily married, happily with children, happily in your community and to feel useful I think is what writing is about. You ought to make people feel better as a result of having read your work, to think, I would like to be like that heroine, or wouldn't it be lovely if my marriage was like

> that. I'm not bothered about people who write about psychopaths and murder. I don't even like detective stories, romances are better than detective stories. At least a girl gets a glimpse of what Sebastian could be like. Okay, poor old Fred, his feet smell a bit, but if you get Fred to lose a few pounds he could be a bit more like Sebastian. I like books to end with the birth of a baby.

Juri Gabriel, who runs two courses at Morley College in South London – one on novel writing, and one that is more general and covers non-fiction as well as fiction – has generated an entirely different atmosphere. His recruits tend to be graduates, and he describes the course as at 'really a postgraduate level'. He attracts more men than women, and finds – as does Target – that some people return year after year. People come, he says, to test out their writing, to get a sense of the general direction in which they should go, and for social reasons.

Gabriel tends to act as a low-key arbiter of group discussions, in which 'the objective standard is publication'. He finds it a real problem that a group ethos has developed which no single individual has any hope of changing. His group's ethos is clearly intellectual, and 'smart literary fiction' receives the best response. Several members and ex-members have published novels, most notably Robert Irwin, who writes for Penguin.

'Nobody writes about feelings,' Gabriel laments. His course might be ideal for would-be thriller writers, but would probably seem hostile territory to a romance writer.

So, too, might a university course like the MA in Creative Writing at the University of East Anglia, which is taught by Malcolm Bradbury and Rose Tremain among others. Janet Hutcheon went on the course after she had tried writing romances:

> The stuff I put in was absolutely lambasted to begin with because it was fairly ordinary, conventional stuff. And anyone who was doing something really imaginative, even if it didn't work, was given encouragement – I was absolutely amazed at the first bits that came through. I thought, what is this? I can't make anything of it. But then as the course goes on you see what people are trying to do, and it stimulates you to be more imaginative and to fly a

> kite now and again. I think it did a lot of good in that way. Otherwise I would be pegged down very much on a prosaic level, and at least I know now what I think I ought to be trying to achieve, even if I don't get it.
>
> But it does have a disadvantage in that it's an academic course so it tends to, for the duration of the course, push you in that direction. I think you even have to come down to earth with a bump afterwards, and reassess it all, and decide for yourself where you need to be really, because I think if you do write like that all the time nobody's going to publish you. Unless you're brilliant, unless you're a really clever born writer, and I don't think I'm that.

Kathy Page, another UEA course graduate, found much the same:

> Although they wouldn't stop anyone writing a straight bodice ripper if that's what they'd started doing, they are most pleased if you do something more adventurous. They do say that there isn't a sort of "school" novel, but I think in a way they are encouraging a certain kind of awareness of what writing has done, and want you to do something with that – on top of it.

Hutcheon had previously been on writing weekends (the UEA course is one year, full time) and found them less satisfactory:

> They were quite fun to do, but I didn't think that any of the women – mostly women – were interested in writing in the way that I wanted to do it. They wrote poetry, articles and magazine stories, and the great thing was how they'd love to write a novel. It was all immensely way out there and you knew they'd probably never get to it. Mostly it was a social occasion. A few writers there were quite successful and had published a lot of books, but they were a class apart.

This is another common problem with writers' groups: that often there is a very high proportion of writers who are not only unpublished, but have little serious expectation of becoming published. Publication might be the objective standard in Gabriel's class, but in other classes there is a clear reluctance to judge work that is submitted at all. The emphasis is on freeing inhibitions and encouraging people to express themselves, rather than on being honest about the shortcomings of their work.

Poet Hilary Mellon's Creative Writing Workshop in Norwich works on these lines. It is an all-women class, and Mellon sets homework exercises each week – for example, asking members to write a short story that opens with a specific sentence, or a poem on a specific theme. Mellon's aim is to have members 'discover their own hidden talents', and the group ethos is oriented towards praise, not criticism. Though this type of class is enjoyable for many amateur writers, the piece-a-week format doesn't foster the long-term planning and revision of book projects, and though the course could give valuable encouragement to uncertain writers, it wouldn't help them to pinpoint their shortcomings.

Revision

How much revision to do is a sensitive topic with writers, not least because of the power of two opposing images. First, there's the idea of the inspired writer who turns out their masterpiece at top speed without a single word change; then there's the image of the painstaking craftsman who emphasizes that they read a thousand books while researching, and rewrote the ending 95 times.

There's no merit in revision for its own sake: work only needs revising if it needs improving. That said, almost any piece of writing can be improved through revision.

You may need to revise on several levels, and it's not easy to do them at the same time. I'd suggest that you do the following – either alone, or with the help of others who are prepared to advise and criticize.

First, read through your entire typescript or synopsis and consider its overall content and balance. Does it work as a whole? In non-fiction, is the content well distributed or are there crowded passages and flat passages? In fiction, does it build up in a pattern of small and large climaxes, or is it too dull and even in tone? Are there boring parts? (It's best if you ask somebody else to tell you this.)

Getting the shape right is one of the hardest things about writing, and it's much more difficult for an editor to correct than is the occasional clumsy sentence. You can only achieve it by reading through the work as a whole, and mentally standing back to consider it as a whole. Don't try to combine this type of revision with sentence-by-sentence revision.

Next, take the book chapter by chapter – or scene by scene, if it is fiction. In non-fiction, ask yourself what you are trying to put across in the chapter. Is all the necessary material included? Is the order sensible, so that the reader is carried easily from one point to the next?

Every scene (and linking passage) in a novel should be there for a purpose. There should be some kind of motive force behind it: something that the reader finds out, some way in which the story is carried forward. It's the setting and resolution of little dilemmas or puzzles that keeps your readers turning the pages.

Look at each scene and ask yourself, why is this scene included? What about it is going to make the reader read on? Does it start at the right point, and end at the right point? Is there a good blend of narrative, description and dialogue, or could you improve the blend?

Look critically at long chunks of descriptive writing. Description slows things down. Try to avoid more than one paragraph of description at a time. Too much detail can overload your readers: a couple of well-chosen touches often bring a character alive far better than a half-page run-down of their every item of clothing.

Your story will be more readable if you try to avoid purely descriptive passages, and provide all the necessary details in the course of the narrative. You shouldn't ever need to digress from your story to tell the reader: 'Mary was 24, with long brown hair and green eyes.'

Instead, you need something like this: 'Mary tossed back her long brown hair. "No I'm not too old to enter the beauty contest," she retorted, scowling at her mother.'

Look critically, too, at long explanatory passages. The rule of good storytelling is to show your readers what's happening and what your characters are thinking and feeling, not to tell them. In other words, don't say: 'Mary was very angry. She wished George would go away.'

Let your reader deduce that, by writing, say: 'Mary turned

her back on George. ''What an absolute pig you are'', she muttered.'

Look carefully at the viewpoint from which you describe the scene. Through whose eyes does your reader learn what is happening? Impersonal narration doesn't work as well as a narration that focuses the reader's attention on one character at a time. Interest in your characters, and a desire to know what happens to them, is what involves your readers with your story. So instead of writing: 'George and Henry turned their backs on each other. Slowly, they began to pace out twenty yards' try something like: 'Henry turned his back on George, and began to count under his breath as he paced out twenty yards. He could hear George's footsteps echoing his own, and could feel the pistol cool and heavy in his hand. He took a deep breath and turned round.'

Do this repeatedly, and the reader will (unless you're being very clever, or very clumsy) rejoice if Henry wins his duel, and mourn if he loses. Describe everything from an Olympian height, and the reader won't care what happens to either Henry or George.

When you have the content of the book right on this level, you need to take a look at your wording and phrasing.

Take each sentence, one by one. Does it say, unambiguously, what you intended it to say? If so, forget the meaning and consider the form. (If not, scrap it and write down precisely what you did intend to say.)

Is it elegant or clumsy? No writing needs to be clumsy. Rephrase it if it is. Is every word needed? Good writing is generally light on adjectives and adverbs: look at each one and consider whether it is really needed. Prune unnecessary words. Don't write 'George shouted angrily,' unless a simple 'George shouted,' really leaves the reader doubting, in context, whether George is angry (and s/he needs to know). Don't even write 'George shouted,' if the reader can deduce that 'You stupid idiot,' is George's line.

Avoid empty adjectives like 'good' and 'nice'. In dialogue, avoid meaningless phrases like 'Oh well,' and 'Isn't it?' Good dialogue is crisper and sounds perfectly naturalistic without them.

Avoid passive constructions unless you are aiming for a specific effect that requires them. 'The candle was lit by George,' is more long-winded and less immediate than 'George lit the candle.'

Avoid using long words where shorter ones will do. Avoid jargon. ('They confronted each other,' not 'They were in a confrontation situation.') Avoid clichés like 'An icy hand gripped her heart,' and 'He was on top of the world.' You can and must find a more original way of conveying the same information.

Watch out for specific words and phrases that you over-use. For example, I have a tendency to use 'and then' a great deal. I read all through my typescripts specifically looking for this combination, and trying to excise it wherever possible. In my last novel, I found I over-used the adjective 'mild' and adverb 'mildly', so I did another specific revision to locate and reconsider each incidence of them.

In summary, there are four levels on which you may need to revise your text:

- your choice of words;
- the phrasing of your sentences;
- the content of individual scenes or sections;
- the overall balance and content of the book.

Look at each of these consciously and separately, and you'll produce a much better quality text.

Computerized assistance

If you have a word processor (and I strongly advise you to get one if you can afford it: it makes revision much less of a chore) then you will probably have access to a spelling checker. Do use it. Even the best speller makes the occasional typing mistake.

Some up-market word processors also incorporate a thesaurus. This can be a great help in encouraging you to expand your vocabulary, and say what you mean more precisely, and with more originality. A thesaurus in book form does the same job, but it's much harder work to use. If you never use Roget, do try a computer thesaurus, and you'll be amazed.

While spelling checkers and thesauruses are now well-established tools, the suggestion of computerized style checking still tends to provoke a hollow laugh. There are fewer style checking programs available, and the general standard and ease of use is below that of word processors and spelling checkers. But these, too, can be extremely helpful tools when it comes to improving your prose – or your poetry, come to that.

A style checker (*Grammatik* is the best known, and the best I've come across) can do any or all of these things for you:

- Pinpoint over-used vocabulary.
- Draw your attention to some undesirable or ungrammatical sentence constructions – for instance, sentences with no verb, split infinitives, and instances of the passive tense.
- Pinpoint jargon, 'empty' words (absolutely, really, nice, etc.), common redundancies (e.g. 'descend down'), sexist phrases and clichés.

These simple suggestions can make a great difference to the readability of your prose. Another related class of programs, of which *Readability* is the best example, analyses the length of your words and sentences to produce an index of its readability, usually based in some way on the Fogg Index. With careful study, this can help you to modify your prose style for the better.

Publishing yourself

A more drastic solution of the problem of repeated rejections is to publish your own work.

Is it worth it? It depends on your motives for wishing to be published. Some writers find that self-publishing suits them well, while others become frustrated by the amount of work involved, the difficulty of finding distributors, and the lack of critical attention for their books.

Poet and artist Pippa King has always published her own books of poems: she has now produced five of varying sizes. She publishes as The Finger Press, and distributes her work to friends, via local bookshops, and at poetry readings:

> *Letters from a Stone Garden* got reviewed in the *Eastern Daily*

> *Press* along with Wendy Cope's *Making Cocoa for Kingsley Amis*. I got very serious letters from people all over the world. Someone wrote to me from Japan, addressed to The Finger Press. I was terribly impressed by it. Jarrolds [a local bookshop] had it and they sold all three copies, and I got a request from a public library to have one, so somewhere there's a bound copy in a public library. But I don't really market them, just produce them.

King clearly enjoys producing her books, and she has learned to keep her print runs small (never more than 500 copies). But her main reason for self-publishing is that 'when it comes to it there's actually nothing else one can do'. She has sent some of her poems to poetry magazines, but she admits to hating the high rejection rate, and hers is a conscious decision to stay outside the mainstream poetry market and develop her own small audience.

Gerda Mayer has also published her own poetry, but unlike King she did so as a stepping-stone to publication elsewhere. (And successfully: her latest collection, *A Heart-ache of Grass*, was published by Peterloo Poets.) She made a deliberate attempt to make the results look throwaway as she was very aware that self-publication is frowned on by many serious poets, and she might subsequently have to 'live it down'.

'I bought an ancient duplicator and, at considerable risk to my dining-room curtains, and with an enormous waste of paper, produced a nine-page stapled booklet. It was originally priced at two pence. After a massive reduction, it came free of charge and went very well.'

Neither King nor Mayer expected to make money out of self-publication – and they didn't.

Psychologist and graphic designer Patricia Brooks tried self-publishing on a larger scale. When she found difficulty in getting a publisher for *The Anatomy of Intelligence*, which she admits goes against the accepted beliefs of the psychological establishment, she decided to produce the book herself. She had 4,000 copies printed, used a professional distributor and a public relations expert, and advertised relatively widely in specialist magazines and journals.

Brooks' main interest was in establishing 'scientific priority' for her ideas, and she feels her book was noticed and reviewed sufficiently to achieve this. Commercially it was not a success, and she eventually had 2,000 copies pulped, rather than continue to pay warehousing charges.

Other self-publishing efforts fare better commercially. Pauline Kirk was part of a group that produced a local history book called *Bramley: the Village that Disappeared*. With a well-defined market, it was sold in local shops, pubs, libraries and cafes, and the print run sold out completely. Kathy Page was involved in another community publishing venture:

> It was a mixture of short stories and poetry. We had lunch with people from Faber & Faber, but they said the combination was a bad idea, so in the end we did it ourselves. It was really satisfying. Very difficult on the distribution front, that was the hardest bit. The production was reasonably costly but relatively easy.
>
> We started off going around bookshops offering sale or return, as many as we could, and doing mail order. Then we got a distributor and they did quite well for a while and then it tailed off. But we just about broke even.

Gael Lindenfield made two attempts at self-publishing, both successfully. *Problem Solving Through Self Help Groups*, written with Robert Adams, was sold through mail order: it had a clearly defined potential audience. The edition of 1,000 copies sold out. Lindenfield subsequently wrote *Assert Yourself*, a book with a wider potential readership which her husband took round to local bookshops. This too sold out. Subsequently she offered the book to Thorsons, rather than attempt to reprint herself, and they published it on a more commercial scale, again with great success.

With the increasing availability of cheap desk-top publishing facilities, self-publishing is becoming a boom sector. If you want to succeed, it's advisable to be realistic about your likely sales, and to research printing and distribution methods before you commit yourself. Very few self-published books become bestsellers, and many booksellers, particularly the larger chains, will not deal with this type of material. Many self-publishers do not even break even, and I do not advise you to embark on self-publishing with the idea that you will make money out of it.

Conclusion

Writing for publication is a profession, and there's an enormous amount to be learned about it. I've only begun to hint at some of the issues to be considered in this short book. There are suggestions for further reading in the Bibliography, and addresses of useful organizations in the Appendix. But there's no short-cut, and no real substitute, for reading a lot, getting plenty of practice at writing, and taking a professional attitude to every aspect of the operation.

Bibliography

There are two essential reference books for freelance writers, both published in annually updated editions. You will certainly need to buy one or both of them:

Writers' and Artists' Yearbook, (A. & C. Black) is the older-established, solid and fact-filled.

The Writer's Handbook, ed. Barry Turner (Macmillan) is a newer, slightly more anecdotal rival.

Other basic reference material for writers (not including general dictionaries, thesauruses and the like):

The Oxford Dictionary for Writers and Editors (OUP) is a guide to spelling, punctuation, capitalization, abbreviations, etc.

Hart's Rules for Compositors and Readers (OUP) contains advice on capitalization, hyphenation, indexing, punctuation marks, etc.

Research for Writers, Ann Hoffmann (A. & C. Black) is a very solid guidebook to sources and methods.

Book Indexing, M. D. Anderson (CUP) is one of a series of short authors' and publishers' guides.

Fowler's Modern English Usage, H. W. Fowler (OUP) is the standard guide to grammatical niceties.

On business aspects of writing, good guides are:

An Author's Guide to Publishing, Michael Legat (Hale). A thorough, fact-filled book which covers everything from submitting work to complaints from authors about publishers.

The Successful Author's Handbook, Gordon Wells (Macmillan/Papermac) is a practical guide mainly for writers of non-fiction handbooks and technical books.

The Business of Freelancing, Graham Jones (BFP Books), though intended mainly for writers of articles and photography, is full of practical information on the business side of working as a freelance writer.

On self-publishing and desktop publishing:

The Writer's Guide to Desktop Publishing, Kathy Lang (Harcourt Brace Jovanovich/Academic Press). A clear guide to the computing side, does not cover distribution and marketing.

How to Publish Yourself, Peter Finch (Allison & Busby) is chatty and informative.

Two publishers produce excellent series of books on aspects of writing:

Allison & Busby, with titles including *The Book Writer's Handbook* (Gordon Wells), *The Craft of Novel-Writing* (Dianne Doubtfire) and *How to Write for Children* (Tessa Krailing).

Elm Tree Books, whose titles include *The Way to Write* (John Fairfax and Joan Moat), *The Way to Write Novels* (Paddy Kitchen) and *The Way to Write Crime Fiction* (Lisanne Radice).

To Writers with Love, Mary Wibberley (Buchan & Enright) is a classic guide for writers of romantic fiction.

Non-fiction: A Guide to Writing and Publishing, David St John Thomas (David & Charles), though slightly dated now, is still the best guide to this specialist field.

Also mentioned in the text:

Reading the Romance: Women, Patriarchy and Popular Literature, Janice A. Radway (Univ. of N. Carolina Press) contains a detailed analysis of readers' responses to romantic fiction.

My Appointment with the Muse, Paul Scott (Heinemann) includes 'Imagination in the Novel' and a variety of other essays and lectures.

The Society of Authors (address in Appendix) produce a series of *Quick Guides* for writers. All are useful, and No. 8, *Publishing Contracts*, is indispensible.

UK Periodicals:

The Author, the Society of Authors' quarterly, provides detailed information (including comments on the performance of individual publishers) as well as general articles of interest.

The Bookseller (weekly) provides some interesting insights into publishers' views of the sales potential of their books.

Appendix: useful addresses

The two major writers' trade unions in the UK are:

The Society of Authors
84 Drayton Gardens
London SW10 9SB
Tel. 071 373 6642

The Writers' Guild of Great Britain
430 Edgware Road
London W2 1EH
Tel. 071 723 8074

In Australia, the equivalents are:

The Australian Society of Authors
22 Alfred Street
Milsons Point
NSW 2061
Tel. 92–7235

Australian Writers' Guild Ltd
60/60A Kellett Street
Kings Cross
NSW 2011
Tel. 326–1900

In Canada:

Canadian Authors' Association
121 Avenue Road
Suite 104
Toronto, Ontario M5R 2G3
Tel. 416–926 8084

The Writers' Union of Canada
The Writers' Centre
24 Ryerson Avenue
Toronto, Ontario M5T 2P3
Tel. 416–868 6913

Similar organizations exist in many other countries: consult the *Writers' and Artists' Yearbook*, local publications or local arts authorities for addresses.

To register for Public Lending Right in the UK, contact:

The Public Lending Right Office
Bayheath House
Prince Regent Street
Stockton-on-Tees
Cleveland TS18 1DF
Tel. 0642 604699

and for German PLR (payable to UK authors):

Authors' Licensing and Collecting Society
7 Ridgmount Street
London WC1E 7AE
Tel. 071 580 2181

Evening and daytime courses for writers of fiction and non-fiction are arranged in the UK by many Local Education Authorities and by the Workers' Educational Association; and by broadly equivalent organizations in other countries. Short residential courses are held by:

The Arvon Foundation
Totleigh Barton
Sheepwash
Beaworthy
Devon EX21 5NS
Tel. 040922 338

A second Arvon Foundation centre is at:
Lumb Bank
Hebden Bridge
West Yorks HX7 6DF
Tel. 0422 843714

Finally, the international writers' organization, P.E.N. International, has an international centre at:

38 King Street
London WC2E 8JT
Tel. 071 379 7939

and its English Centre at:

7 Dilke Street
London SW3 4JE
Tel. 071 352 6303
with additional centres in many other countries throughout the world.

Acknowledgements

My grateful thanks are due to all the authors, literary agents and editors who discussed their experiences with me and allowed me to quote their comments and advice in this book. As well as those named herein, I'm indebted to Peter Sansom, Caroline Price, Joe Rothman, Lotte Kramer, John Priestley, and numerous other writer acquaintances present and past.

Thanks, too, to the friends and acquaintances who helped me to track down authors, most notably Myra Schneider, Andrew Best of Curtis Brown, Kate Allen of Thorsons and Tessa Shapcott of Mills & Boon; and to Mark Le Fanu of the Society of Authors.

Index